How to Sell on eBay for Beginners

eBay Learning Series Book 1

Steve Nichols

Copyright © 2020 Steve Nichols
All Rights Reserved

Table of Contents

What's Selling on eBay Right Now? 1
Why You Need To Read This Book 3
Introduction 4
Chapter 1: Can A New Seller Make Money On Ebay? 6
Chapter 2: Account Set-Up and Selling Fees 10
Chapter 3: What You Need to Get Started 16
Chapter 4: Sourcing Inventory 20
Chapter 5: Research 30
Chapter 6: Getting Ready To List 36
Chapter 7: Listing Your Items For Sale 45
Chapter 8: Packing And Shipping 58
Chapter 9: Opening An Ebay Store 73
Chapter 10: Seller Performance Standards 76
Chapter 11: Managing Your Ebay Business 78
Chapter 12: You Can't Sell It If They Can't Find It 95
Chapter 13: Treasure Tales: $55.00 To $4025.00 98
Chapter 14: Stuff I Thought You Should Know 101
Conclusion 105
About The Author 107

What's Selling on eBay Right Now?

The simple answer: Mobile phones and accessories. It's been the best selling category for years.

Here's a list of the best selling eBay items during COVID-19:

- Puzzles
- Strength Training
- Webcams
- Painting Equipment and Supplies
- Cardio Equipment
- Laptop Docking Stations and Power Adapters
- Golf Training Aids
- Wireless Routers and Mobile Hotspots
- VR Headsets
- Lego Building Toys

But this is a book for *beginning* eBay sellers. You probably don't have any of those things lying around the house, and unless you have the means to start an eBay business selling mobile phones and accessories, you should probably start close to home, with items you can find at yard sales, estate sales and auctions. For new sellers, I recommend vintage or used collectibles.

Here's an eBay search you can do to see what's selling in those categories right now.

You'll need to have an eBay account for this search. After you've logged in, find the *"Advanced"* link at the top of the page. It's just to the right of the blue search button. Then follow these steps:

1. Click "Advanced"

2. In the box under, **Enter Keywords or item number**, enter "vintage" without the quotes.

3. From the **In this category** menu select "Collectibles"

4. Below the blue search button put a check in the box next to "Sold Listings."

5. Scroll down to the **Condition** section and put a check in the box next to "Used."

6. Then scroll back up and click the blue search button.

What you see now is a list of sold items that sellers have described as vintage, used, and listed in one of the collectible categories. The search results show the most recent sold listings first. Study this list to get ideas.

Why You Need to Read This Book

I've been selling on eBay for more than 21 years. I joined in March, 1999 and started out just selling stuff I had around the house. I worked full time driving a local delivery truck while doing eBay part time. This is not a book full of theory. What you'll find here are examples and tips from the real world of selling on eBay. I've made all the mistakes and figured most of this out on my own.

I've sold everything from coins to a vintage jukebox on eBay. I've been a Top-Rated seller for the past 9 years and maintained 100% feedback and a 4.9 out of 5-star rating as of this writing. I'm a former eBay Education Specialist trained by eBay to help new sellers learn to sell on eBay. eBay discontinued the Education Specialist Program a few years ago, but I still enjoy helping people learn how to sell on eBay. That's why I wrote this book.

Introduction

Just 10 years ago (2010), eBay had about 90 million active users. Today that number has grown to 182 million. This means there's a lot more competition and you're competing with a lot of other sellers to sell your items. But it also means more buyers.

I frequently refer to eBay selling fees and policies, and I've spent a lot of time doing research to make sure everything you read here is up to date.

There are no illustrations or pictures in this book. It's best to be on your computer or eBay app when going through topics like setting up your account and doing searches.

The eBay Mobile App

About 35% of all mobile phone users have downloaded the eBay mobile app. The eBay app is the third most popular shopping app behind Amazon and Wal-Mart, and about 60% of all eBay purchases are made with a mobile device. Buying from your smartphone is different than with a computer. The listings look different. You *must* have your listings set up so mobile shoppers can find them, which means using a lot of *item specifics*. I cover this later. Plenty of good pictures are extremely important, especially for buyers using the app. eBay does not make it easy to read the item description on the mobile app. Buyers only see a small portion unless they click through to read everything, and the part of the description they do see is not usually the beginning of the text.

You won't find a tutorial about how to list and sell with the eBay mobile app in this book. I use it for research when I'm sourcing and to monitor my sales and messages. A lot of sellers use the app exclusively for all their eBay work and that's okay. I prefer to use a computer because it's the set up I've used for a long time and it works well for me.

There are lots of examples in this book. I believe it makes the material much easier to understand, like the board game everyone had to have for Christmas 2018.

Monopoly for Millennials was the hot item for Christmas 2018. In November I was able to find ten of these at Wal-Mart for about $22.00 each including tax. I sold them all on eBay pretty quickly for about $60.00 each plus shipping. After fees and supplies, I made a profit of about $275.00 in less than 2 weeks. I kept one for myself, and we had a blast playing it at Thanksgiving.

Chapter 1

Can a New Seller Make Money on eBay?

Do you want a part time business that you can work from home and set your own hours? Maybe you want to turn it into a full-time business. Whatever your goal, know this: it's not easy. Your success depends on how much time you put into learning and working the business. If you're just looking to sell some stuff around your house, there are a lot of other ways to do it. You can have a yard sale or sell it on Facebook Marketplace. Answering these questions will help you decide how far you want to go with eBay.

There is still a **huge** market on eBay for vintage goods, antiques and collectibles. For many of these things, eBay is really the best and sometimes the only choice. For example, I recently picked up a vintage Freddy Krueger collectible lighter at a yard sale for one dollar. I listed it on eBay and it sold 3 or 4 days later for $17.99. No one is going to Amazon looking for a vintage Freddy Krueger Nightmare on Elm Street lighter. Sure, you could put it on FB Marketplace or Craigslist and it might eventually sell. But why not put it in front of millions of potential buyers, sell it for more money, pack it and drop it off at the post office?

It's possible to go to a few yard sales on a Saturday, spend ten or twenty dollars then list those things on eBay and turn it into a hundred dollars very quickly. I have done it many times, and it's still a great way to make some extra money.

Be a Buyer First

Maybe you've already decided that you want to sell on eBay and need help. You might do some research, read a few books and decide it's not for you. You may already have an eBay account and a PayPal account. If so, and if you have already bought stuff on eBay, you're ahead of the game. You know how eBay works.

If you've never bought anything on eBay, I suggest registering for eBay and setting up a PayPal account. Browse the eBay site and find some inexpensive things like books, DVDs or other inexpensive items. It won't take long to get the hang of navigating the eBay site. When I'm looking for something specific, I enter what I'm looking for in the eBay search bar at the top of any page.

Here's a search you can try: Enter "apple iPhone" into the search bar. I just did this and the search returned over 94,000 listings. Down the left side of the page, under "Categories" are some links. On my search, the third item down the list, "Cell Phones & Smartphones", is in bold letters. This is the category that eBay thinks is most relevant to my search. You can narrow your search for a specific carrier by clicking one of the boxes under "network". Below that is model, storage capacity, etc. The first two categories shown in my search are "Cell Phones & Accessories", and "Cell Phone Accessories". When I click on "Cell phones and accessories", I get over 21,000,000 results. Experiment with it and see what you come up with. Enter some other items into the search bar. Always notice all the information on the left. The links are categories. There are bold headings with lists of items below them. These are *item specifics*. You narrow a search by checking those boxes. Filling in the item specifics is very important when making an eBay listing. This is how buyers search, and eBay is moving closer to making item specifics mandatory in your listings. The more item specifics in your listing, the greater chance you have of it being seen. I'll cover all this in the section on listing your item for sale.

There are three ways you can buy an item on eBay. They are Auctions, Buy It Now, and Best Offer.

Auctions

When eBay started, this was the only way you could buy on the site. Auctions only make up about 10 to 15 percent of eBay sales now. Some auctions may also have a "Buy it now" button at the top of the page. Sellers can choose to add this to auction listings if there's a price they're willing to accept right away.

Buy It Now

Most of eBay purchases today are Buy It Now. This is called Fixed Price Listings when listing your item for sale. All you do is click on the "Buy it now" button and make payment.

Buy It Now with Best Offer

eBay listings that offer this will have a blue "Make an Offer" button near the top of the page. You click on this button and enter your offer price. The seller can choose to accept, decline, or counter your offer. If the offer is accepted, the listing is ended and you are obligated to pay just the same as if you had clicked on buy it now.

Take some time and browse the site. If you're not ready to register, you can still purchase as a guest, you just won't be able to leave feedback for the seller. Buy a couple of inexpensive things to get some experience buying and paying. When the packages arrive take a close look at how the items are packed and what kind of packing materials are used.

I sold vintage magazine advertisements for while. I would buy boxes of old Life magazines at flea markets and remove full page ads to sell on eBay. Before listing them, I ordered a couple from different sellers to see how they packaged them.

Chapter 2

Account Set-Up and Selling Fees

The eBay site has all the information you need to get your account set up, so I don't see the need to repeat that info here. I don't put many links in my books because it's frustrating for readers if the links don't work. You can type most anything into Google like, *"how to set up an eBay selling account",* and the link you see should take you straight to the correct page on the eBay site. You'll have the option of setting up a personal or business account. If you're going to be doing any selling at all, I recommend setting up a business account. The only difference between the two during the initial set up is that you will enter a business name and some other details like type of business and your address. Your business name can be anything you want to put there. Before you can list your first item for sale, you must add an automatic payment method to pay your eBay fees. You can pay your fees with PayPal or with direct debit or credit card. I recommend setting up a PayPal account if you don't have one. This way, money you collect from your sales will go into your PayPal account, and you can use those funds to pay your eBay fees.

Setting up Your PayPal Account

Go to paypal.com and click "sign up" in the upper right corner.

Select "Business Account" on the next page and follow the instructions. Go to the eBay customer service page, "Getting Paid with PayPal", for all the information you need for setting up your listings to accept PayPal and for linking your eBay and PayPal accounts.

eBay Managed Payments

By the end of 2020, most eBay sellers will be moved to eBay Managed Payments meaning you won't need Paypal to collect your sales. The fees are cheaper than PayPal, and they're added to your invoice. So instead of PayPal collecting their fees at the time of the sale, you don't pay these fees till your next invoice.

Managed payments give buyers more ways to pay and it should be better for sellers. There are a few differences. Money from your sales goes straight into your bank account instead of PayPal. eBay transfers money to your account every day, but the money isn't available immediately. It usually takes a couple of days. You'll still print shipping labels as usual, and the money is deducted from your payout.

Your Seller Hub

When you log in to eBay you'll see a page that looks like eBay's home page but it will have links at the top like "My eBay", "Sell", and at the top left, a link that says "Hi", followed by your first name. The easiest way to manage all your selling activity is eBay's Seller Hub. The Seller Hub overview page summarizes all you need to know about your selling activity. There are 6 tabs at the top of Seller Hub that access a range of tools and data. They are: **Overview, Orders, Listings, Marketing, Performance**, and **Research**. For sellers using Managed Payments there is another tab called **Payments.**

The two sections I use most are **Overview** and **Listings.** Overview gives you access to pending tasks, sales data, orders data, all your listing data, traffic data, handy shortcuts, selling tools and more.

The **Listings** tab has links to your active listings, unsold listings and others. This data is also accessible from the overview page below the tasks section.

To use Seller Hub, you'll need to have had at least one sale. For some reason, eBay doesn't make Seller Hub easy to find from their site. It's not even included in the site map. To get to the seller hub Google "eBay seller hub." My seller hub is bookmarked and saved in my toolbar.

What About the eBay Fees?

eBay charges two main types of selling fees: an insertion fee when you create a listing and a final value fee when your item sells. You don't pay these fees in advance. eBay will debit your payment method each month for selling fees owed for the prior month's sales. If you have an eBay store subscription, the subscription fee is billed in advance. To see what the current eBay selling fees are, I recommend checking the fees section on the eBay website. eBay gives you a set number of free insertions each month, and then charges a fee per insertion (or per listing) for each one over the number of free insertions. The per insertion fees usually range from .05 to .35 per listing depending on whether or not you have an eBay store and what type of store you have. I cover eBay stores in detail in chapter 9. eBay gives you 50 free insertions each month if you don't have a store subscription.

You're charged a final value fee based on the total amount of the sale including shipping. Final value fees are 10% of the total sale for most items. Books, DVDs and music (except records) are 12% of the total sale at the time of this writing. When I say the total sale, that means the sale price of your item *plus* the actual shipping cost that is paid by the buyer.

Why does eBay charge a final value fee on shipping? This question is asked a lot in Facebook groups. When eBay started, you only paid fees on the *selling price* of the item. The answer is simple: sellers were trying to avoid paying selling fees. Say you had an item worth $50.00 and it cost $5.00 to ship. Sellers would avoid final value fees by making the selling price something like $2.00 and the shipping cost would be $53.00. You still had the same total cost, but now sellers were only paying fees on $2.00 and not the actual selling price. eBay quickly caught on to this and decided to charge a final value fee on the total, including shipping.

There are several optional listing upgrade fees designed to enhance your listings and make them stand out. I personally don't use them and don't think it's worth the extra money. For example, to add a bold title to your listing, you will pay $4.00 extra for a fixed price listing or $2.00 extra for an auction.

PayPal Fees

In addition to eBay selling fees, you also have PayPal fees. PayPal charges you for their service of processing the payment. Unlike eBay fees, the PayPal fees are collected when the sale is made. The PayPal fees are 30 cents per transaction and 2.9% of the total sale including shipping. PayPal deducts their part first and puts the balance in your account immediately. If you're a new seller and have a new PayPal account, your payments may be held until you establish a history of shipping on time. PayPal will typically hold funds for up to 21 days or until tracking shows the item delivered. Shipping labels printed through eBay or PayPal should automatically update and release your funds as soon as tracking shows the item delivered. How do you pay for shipping if PayPal is holding your money? Cost of shipping is released to your account shortly after purchase is made so you can have funds available to ship. However, it's a good idea to have a credit or debit card linked to your PayPal account as a back-up funding source. Once you establish a history of reliable service, this should not be a problem.

Sales Taxes

eBay handles all the sales taxes for sellers. They charge buyers sales tax based on the state they live in. eBay collects the sales tax and pays it to the states. As sellers there is nothing we need to do regarding sales tax. You do not pay fees to eBay for the amount of sales tax collected. PayPal, however, collects fees based on the *entire* transaction, including sales tax. PayPal is a payment processor. A business that takes credit cards pays the credit card company a percentage of the entire transaction. It's simply a cost of doing business. If you have a sale of $50.00 including shipping and the sales tax is 10 percent, you're talking about less than two cents. This is a bargain considering you don't have the headache of collecting sales taxes and keeping records for every state you sell to.

Example Fee Calculation

Here's a breakdown of the fees you would pay if you sold a smartphone for $400.00 with free shipping.

eBay fees – 10% or $40.00

PayPal fees - .30 + 2.9% or $11.90

Total fees -$40.00 + $11.90= $51.90, or about $52.00 in fees.

If you're still within your 50 free insertions for the month, then it will cost you $52.00 in fees to sell this phone.

I didn't include the PayPal fees for sales tax in this example. That would vary by state. If you ship to a buyer in Tennessee, the extra PayPal fee for collecting sales tax would be 83 cents.

Chapter 3

What You Need to Get Started

A computer is a must have for doing any serious selling on eBay. I use an HP Desktop running Windows 10. You should also have a good working knowledge of computers and the internet. I don't recommend using the eBay app on your smartphone for selling. It doesn't have all the features you need. If you're serious about selling, you need a dedicated space to work, like a desk or table.

Reliable Internet Access

High speed internet or wifi is essential. We have a Comcast bundle that includes TV, landline phone service and internet. My wife works from home in the medical industry. Between us we have 3 desktop computers connected by ethernet, cable TV, two phone lines for my wife's office (fax and phone) and wifi for our Netflix box.

Printer

Your printer depends on the volume of labels you plan to print. I use a Dell v313 printer for all my printing needs and it works just fine for my labels as well. I use the 8.5" x 11" label sheets that have 2 labels per sheet. You can buy these on eBay, at Wal-Mart or any office supply store.

Digital camera

I recommend a digital camera that takes good close up photos (an absolute must). I use a Canon PowerShot. A smart phone with a good camera that takes good close up pictures will work as well, but I personally prefer using a digital camera.

Digital scale

I have a Weigh Max that I have had for over 10 years. You can get one for less than $30 on eBay and they're available at any office supply store. Mine will display weight in pounds, ounces and tenths of an ounce. You must get the weight right for listing anything. I like a scale that shows tenths of an ounce. If the scale shows that your package weighs 9.1 ounces, you must enter the weight as 10 ounces. I'll talk more about packing and shipping later.

Tape Measure

For adding measurements to your listing, estimating box size, and filling in shipping details.

Hand held tape dispenser

I use a simple hand held dispenser that you can buy at any office supply store or Wal-Mart.

Smartphone with the eBay app

This is a game changer. It's a must have tool when you're sourcing inventory. Pop open the eBay app and do a quick search to see what items are selling for. Here's an example of what I'm talking about.

June 6, 2020: I was on my way to Lowe's today, and I passed an inside yard sale about a mile from my house. Yes, it seems the yard sales are coming back. This sale was a fundraiser for an animal shelter right down the road. I found two items, **new in the package** for $5.00 each. One was a Spiderman Build-A-Figure. Using my eBay app, I scanned the barcode and found two *sold* listings for $85.00 and $88.00. The other item was a Sennheiser stereo listening system. I scanned this one and found that one had sold for $99.00.

I paid $10.00 for items worth $180.00 on eBay, and I wasn't even looking for a yard sale. **You can do this!**

Packing Material

You should keep a variety of shipping boxes and padded mailing envelopes on hand. I keep a selection of different sizes of new, plain cardboard boxes and USPS Priority Mail boxes on hand. I also have various sizes of padded mailing envelopes, both plain and post office priority mail. You can get all the priority mail supplies you need, free from the postal service. Local post offices keep some items on hand but they usually don't carry everything you need. You can order these free on the USPS website and have them shipped free to your door.

The other packing supplies you should have on hand are packing peanuts, bubble wrap, packaging tape and regular masking tape. I use a piece of masking tape to tape the bubble wrap in place after wrapping an item. It's much easier for the customer to remove the bubble wrap that way.

Work Area and Storage

At the very least, you should have a designated area to organize and store your inventory. We have a small bedroom that we don't use and I converted that into an office. My desk, files, computer and printer are all set up there. I also have a lot of shelving in my office, some of which is dedicated to storing books and small items I have listed on eBay.

I also recommend a work area for packing and shipping. We have a garage that we don't use as a garage. I have a packing bench in there that has room for my bubble wrap, tape and dispenser on the top. I store shipping boxes on a shelf under the bench. I also have plastic shelving I picked up at Lowe's for storing more packaging and my eBay inventory.

I've been selling on eBay for a long time, so I have a lot of shipping supplies on hand. Sometimes I don't have exactly what I need to ship an odd shaped item, but I'm ready to ship almost anything that comes in.

Chapter 4

Sourcing Inventory

Finding sources of inventory, knowing what to buy and what not to buy is something that takes time to learn. I've been doing this for over 20 years and I still learn something new all the time. The longer you do this the better you'll be at recognizing things of value that you know will sell on eBay.

The first things I listed on eBay were NASCAR collectibles. Take a look around your house and decide what you don't want anymore. The easiest things to sell on eBay are books, CDs and DVDs. Do you have any you don't want? That would be a great place to start. Old toys, games and electronics are also good. I don't recommend trying to sell clothing on eBay when you're starting out. You really need to know what you're doing and clothing has a high return rate on eBay compared to other things and there is *a lot* of competition in this field.

What Sells on eBay?

I try to concentrate on older, vintage and collectible type things that don't have tons of similar listings on eBay. Here is a list of the types of things I look for. I've sold all these things on eBay.

Books: Old cookbooks (especially Betty Crocker), bibles, Harry Potter hardbacks, Hymnals, vintage Sears and J.C. Penny catalogs.

Vintage Electronics: Sony Walkman, 8 track players, 1970s and 80s stereo receivers, portable typewriters, hand held electronic games, programmable calculators, 70s and 80s clock radios, cassette recorders, vintage cameras, especially the Polaroid land camera, and tube radios.

College Textbooks: In my treasure tales later in the book, I tell you how I bought a pick-up load of college textbooks at an auction for $55.00 and turned it into $4025.00 in sales. That was a rare find, but there's a huge market for used college textbooks. If you live near a college, check the thrift stores around there. You can quickly see what they're selling for by scanning the bar code.

Some other things I've sold are vintage office equipment, vintage toys, Star Wars collectibles, old magazines, collectible coffee mugs, old signs, vintage Christmas ornaments, and junk jewelry.

eBay has been around so long and there are so many sellers now that almost anything you see at a yard sale, auction, or estate sale is for sale on eBay. You can do a quick eBay search and get an idea of what it's selling for. The search example at the beginning of the book was for vintage collectibles. If you know what types of items are going to be at a particular sale, you can do some advanced research. Say you're reading an auction or estate sale listing and they advertise that there are a lot of vinyl records for sale. I see old records at almost every auction I go to. Just go to the advanced listing page, enter vinyl record in the keyword search box, select the music category, check *sold listings* and *used condition* and see what you come up with. It's even easier if you can see pictures of some of the items in the sale listing. You can do a search for that specific item.

Most auction companies have a website and each auction will be advertised on the site. Good listings have a lot of pictures and a long list of many of the items for sale. I'm going to one in a few weeks that lists "8 Track Tape Collection, Elvis and Others" as one of the featured items. There are no pictures of the 8-tracks on the page, but they thought it was important to mention that some of them were Elvis. I did an advanced search with the following criteria: Keyword: **8-track**, Category: Music, Search including: **Sold listings** and Condition: **Used**. When the search results page loads, I go to the drop-down menu to the right and select "Highest First" and I can see which 8-tracks are selling for the most money. While there's a good chance that I won't see any of these at the sale, I have an idea of what certain things are selling for. Like the 8-track motion picture soundtrack for "*The Shining*" that just sold for $295.00.

When I add "Elvis" to the search box and do the search again, sorted by highest first, I see that Elvis 8-track tapes of movie soundtracks bring the most money. **HarumScarum**: $199.95, **Clambake**: $150.00, and **Blue Hawaii**: $94.00.

As a rule, there are two items that I don't sell on eBay: glassware and clothing. Clothing has a high return percentage and the market is flooded with used clothing. I don't like really fragile items such as heavy glassware, but I *will* sell in this category if I can find something like collectible coffee mugs. It all depends on what you can find and what you're interested in. If you have expertise in used clothing, then go for it. Just study the eBay listings for items similar to what you want to sell. There are a couple of good books on Amazon about what sells on eBay: "*101 Items to Sell on eBay*" and "*101 More Items to Sell on eBay*" by Ann Eckhart.

Where Do I Find Stuff to Sell?
- Yard Sales and Garage Sales
- Estate Sales
- Church Sales
- Thrift Stores
- Craigslist
- Personal Property Auctions
- Online Auctions
- Storage Unit Auctions
- Auction Houses
- Discount Stores
- ShopGoodwill.com
- Facebook Marketplace

Yard Sales and Garage Sales

You can find some really good stuff at yard sales. They're easy to find. Just drive through your neighborhood on any Friday or Saturday. Join Facebook yard sale groups in your area. Posts in the groups will usually have several pictures of the merchandise. Yard sales are also advertised in newspapers. One of my favorite resources for yard sale listings is gsalr.com. (That's GSALR, **not** GSAIR). This site is nationwide. Enter your zip code and see yard sales close to you. You can search by keyword and save your search criteria. You can also have them email you anytime a yard sale matches your search criteria.

Here's something you need to keep in mind while shopping at yard sales: Most everything you see is already on eBay, probably in hundreds of listings. That doesn't mean you won't find good stuff. I like yard sales because I usually find something I want to keep for myself as well as keeping an eye out for stuff to put on eBay. One day I was at a local grocery store and right across the street from the store I saw a sign for a yard sale down that street. I decided to stop at that sale on the way home. I found a vintage glass milk bottle that I paid $5.00 for and sold it a couple of weeks later on eBay for $25.00 plus shipping. You never know what you'll find.

Here's something I just heard about: It's a site called **VarageSale**, or varagesale.com. It's been around since 2012. Use it to find sales near you. It's a great way to buy and sell!

Estate sales

Estate sales usually run Thursday through Saturday, sometimes on Sunday. They're liquidation sales where the family has removed personal belongings and things they want to keep, and an estate sale company is hired to handle the sale. You can do well at estate sales if you get there early on the first day of the sale. Try to get there an hour or so before the doors are open, because the best stuff goes fast. The estate sale companies in my area actually use eBay to price a lot of items so, for that reason it doesn't work that well for me. The best deals are usually on the second, third or last day of these sales because the items are marked down every day. To find estate sales in your area, go to estatesales.org.

Church sales

I love church sales. They're sometimes called rummage sales. The good thing about these sales is that everything is donated and usually sold very cheap. I have found some good stuff at these sales. There is one church in my area that has a big sale every year. On the last day they always have a "bag sale". You pick up brown paper grocery bags at the door and everything you can put in a bag is $2.00 for the whole bag. People have donated stuff they don't want and the church is doing a fund raiser. They want to get rid of it. As my wife says, "They ain't tryin' to keep it."

Thrift stores

There are eBay sellers that make a six-figure income just from sourcing at thrift stores. Do a Google search for "eBay lavender clothesline". This seller has a YouTube channel full of videos of her actually out shopping at Goodwill and other thrift stores.

Craigslist

This is hit or miss, but I do look at Craigslist a couple of times a week. I'm interested in vintage computers and I like to go to the computer section and type, "vintage" in the search box. A couple of years ago I found a working TRS-80 computer for sale about seven miles from me. The seller even brought it to my house. I paid $80.00 for it and would like to have kept it for myself, but I ended up selling it for over $400.00 on eBay, plus a considerable amount for shipping.

Check the free listings in Craigslist. I once saw a listing for around 100 *For Dummies* books but just didn't have the time to go get them. Keep in mind that the free stuff is not there for long.

Personal Property Auctions

My favorite auctions are the onsite personal property auctions. These are held at the client's home. The estate is usually being liquidated because one or both of the owners have passed away. Typically, everything in the house, with the exception of personal items like pictures and documents, is sold.

The personal property auctions near me are usually held on Saturday mornings at 10:00 am. Everything in the house with the exception of large furniture and appliances is brought outside. The better items are laid out on tables, but most of the items will be in boxes and sold in "box lots".

I talked a little about research above. Most auctions sales will be listed on a website. Study the listing and look at the pictures. Do whatever research you can ahead of time. Make notes of what you are interested in and how much you're willing to pay.

On auction day, you should plan to get there at least an hour before auction time. This will give you time to register and look at everything offered for sale. The auction listing page only has room to show you a fraction of what is available at the sale. Usually, the best buys will be the things that you don't see in the sale listing. I usually try to arrive 90 minutes before the scheduled time to get a good parking place. I have been to a lot of auctions where the only place to park was along a narrow street. The first time you have to carry a pile of stuff half a mile to your vehicle you'll see what I mean.

When the auction starts, one of the helpers, or "ring men" as they are called, will hold up an item or items to be sold. The auctioneer will open up the bidding. Every auctioneer is different. Some will ask for a starting bid for x amount and keep coming down until a bidder takes the bid. Some will ask the bidders to open the bidding. If you have never been to an auction, you may want to attend one and just watch and learn.

Usually toward the end of the sale, auctioneers will group more and more items together to make sure everything is sold. They may sell a "table deal," or several tables of lower valued items together. If you see something you're interested in but don't want to buy a table full of stuff to get it, ask one of the ring men to sell that item separately. They usually don't mind because they'll most likely end up selling the table full of stuff for the same price anyway.

The best resource to find auctions near you is **auctionzip.com**.

Online Auctions

Online auctions are getting more popular as more people are doing everything from home. Some of the personal property auction companies in my area are doing a lot of online auctions now. They go into the client's home, sort everything into numbered lots and you bid online similar to eBay. The auction will specify a day and time you can go inspect everything. Then, after the auction, you go to the location to pay and pick up your merchandise. A good online source is shopgoodwill.com. See more about it below.

Storage Unit Auctions

"Storage Wars style" storage unit auctions are rarely good for strictly an eBay seller. I owned an antique store for a few years and went to a lot of storage unit auctions.

Auction Houses

These auctions are usually held weekly on Friday or Saturday night. The auction house separates the better items and everything is sold in lots. Lots can be one item or multiple items. The bidders will have time to review everything for sale and will see how items will be grouped for sale. These sales attract mostly people that are buying things to keep, so it's hard to make money from these auctions. Find these sales with auctionzip.com.

Discount Stores

I'm talking about big box stores like Ross, Marshall's, and T.J. Maxx. Right now I have a new Masterclass Premium Cookware skillet listed on eBay for $43.99 that I paid $12.95 plus tax for at T.J.Maxx. My listing currently has 4 watchers at that price. This skillet was originally sold at outlets like Bed, Bath and Beyond for around $100.00, so they sell very well on eBay for half that. Just keep in mind that you'll be competing with a lot of other sellers when sourcing items at these stores.

ShopGoodwill.com

This is a great online resource, but you have a lot of competition. ShopGoodwill.com is run from California and Goodwill stores from all over the country list on the site. They have hundreds of thousands of listings, mostly as seven-day auctions. I know of one eBay seller that does very well selling nothing but used Nerf toys he sources exclusively from ShopGoodwill. You don't need an account to browse the site, but you do need to sign up to buy.

It takes some practice navigating the site to find what you're interested in. There are thousands of items in every category. There are so many, it's hard to look at them all. What I like to do is check the site every day and focus on the items ending that day. That's the best way I've found to see everything in a particular area you might be interested in. Click the "Ending Today" link at the top of the page to see all the listings ending today. I just did a search and it shows over 67,000 listings. Then click the categories menu to start searching for whatever you want to check out.

Facebook Marketplace

Go to Facebook and enter "marketplace" in the search bar. You'll be surprised what you'll find. With smaller items, some sellers will accept PayPal and ship the item to you.

Chapter 5

Research

Before I buy anything, I want to be reasonably sure it will sell on eBay. The easiest way to do this is an eBay search. The eBay app makes it easy to do research while you're out sourcing inventory. Even after years of doing this I still run across something at every sale that I need to do a quick search on.

I was at an auction a couple of years ago and saw two Lord of the Rings Fighting Knives Scabbard sets new in the box. I had never seen one so I did a quick search and found two sold listings, one $225 and the other $250. There was only one unsold listing with a sales price of around $300. Keep in mind that there's a difference between what a seller wants for the item and what it sold for. I found two listings that *sold* for over $200 and I don't know if the other one sold for $300 or not. At personal property auctions like this one, items can be sold individually, in groups of similar items, or in a large lot or table full of unrelated items. In this case, the auctioneer offered both of these as one lot. I was sure I could easily get $200 or more each for these and that they would sell pretty fast. Either there weren't any other eBay sellers there that day or no one else knew the value of these. I opened the bidding at $10.00, the auctioneer asked for $15.00 and another bidder raised his hand. I bid $20.00, and there were no bidders at the next increment of $25.00. I got both of those scabbards for $20 (for both) and sold them for $225.00 each within a week. I made a profit of $365 after fees on just that one twenty dollar purchase.

Note: Here's another example of why I love personal property auctions. You never know what you'll find. I'm actually writing this book on an HP laptop I bought at this very same auction. Price: $27.50.

There are several tools that you can use to determine value and help you decide if something is worth buying to sell on eBay.

eBay Search

eBay searches are done by simply entering a specific item in the search box at the top of any page, or using the advanced search option I talked about before. I'm going to use a specific item as an example. I was in Walgreen's one day and they had a display of Funko Pop figures in one of the aisles. I noticed that one of the boxes said Star Wars on it. I always pay attention to anything that has that Star Wars logo on it. These particular figures were exclusive to Walgreens, so I decided to check it out.

I opened the eBay app on my phone. As soon as the app opens, you see the eBay logo and the search box at the top. As with any iPhone text field, just tap it and enter the search term and click the blue search button at the bottom. If an item is new in the box or is a book or CD, you can use the camera on your phone to scan the barcode. Tap the camera icon at the right of the search box and the bar code scanner will come up. Put the red line over the bar code and you'll get a list of that specific item. These are unsold listings; items currently for sale. At the bottom you should see how many there are, such as 32 results. Sometimes eBay will omit some of the results and only show you what they think is most relevant. I'm not sure how they determine this, but they tell you right at the top that some search results were omitted and they give you a link to click if you want to see all results. At the top there are three links: "Save", meaning you can save this search, "Sort", and "Filter". "Sort" lets you choose the order you want the listings presented. "Best match" is shown by default. You can also have the results listed lowest price to highest, highest to lowest, ending the soonest, newly listed, and by distance from you. Tapping "Filter" will give you a lot of options for refining your search.

For research, I'm only interested in completed listings. Tap "Completed Items" and then "Done". What you see is a list of all the eBay completed listings that match your search. The eBay search only gives you results for the last 90 days. The prices in green are what the items actually sold for, and the prices in red are listings that ended without being sold. There is a lot of information here. It takes experience to be able to look at the search results and decide what the market is for your item. For example, if there were a total of 1000 completed listings and 650 sold listings, you know that 350 of those items did not sell. There can be a lot of reasons for this. There may be too many for sale, or some may have been priced too high. If you think you can price your item at or below the sold listings then you may have a winner. I won't buy anything that I'm not reasonably sure I can sell for at least three times what I paid for it. I prefer to sell it for four times the purchase price, but three times my cost is my limit. It also depends on demand. If an item is in demand and I think it will sell quickly (like within a week), I may even buy a higher priced item that will only sell for twice my purchase price.

If you're on a computer, all the search refinements are along the left side of the search results. Scroll down until you see "Completed listings" and "Sold listings".

Terapeak Research

Terapeak is a research company that was bought by eBay in 2017. It was formerly available as a monthly subscription to research items on Amazon and eBay. It's no longer a standalone service and can only be used for eBay research now. Terapeak is accessed through your "my eBay" page. If you have a Basic, Premium, Anchor or Enterprise Store, Terapeak Research is included free with your subscription. Sellers without an eBay store or with a starter store subscription will pay $19.00 a month for Terapeak. The advantage of Terapeak is that you can search sold listings for up to a full year. All the filters, such as condition and listing format are available, as well as a few others. What I like the most about Terapeak is that it compiles all the data into a summary right at the top of the search results. You can see the total items sold, what the average sold price was, total sales, sell through rate, average shipping cost and what percentage of items had free shipping. There is not a Terapeak smart phone app available any more, but you can always access it with the web browser on your phone. And remember that the Terapeak data only shows you *sold listings*. The sell through rate will give you the percentage of items that sold compared to the total listed, but all the sales data refers to sold items only.

I like to look at sold listings to compare and get ideas. Like a regular eBay search, you can click on links to view the listings, but only the listings sold in the last 90 days. For the rest, you can only see the title and selling price. You'll find the link to Terapeak under the "Research" tab in your seller hub.

Amazon

If I can't find an item on eBay, sometimes I'll search for it on Amazon. This won't work for vintage collectibles and antiques, but if you have a rare book or CD, check prices on Amazon to get an idea. Also, I occasionally like to check Amazon to get an idea of what things are selling for over there.

Other Research Sites

For records and music, **Popsike.com** and **Discogs.com** are two references I like. Popsike is a paid service that costs $18.00 for six months. It is an archive of all vinyl records that have been sold at online auction (the majority of results are from eBay) since 2003. You can sort several different ways including low to high price and high to low. Just be sure to look at several of the results and make sure you're looking at one similar to what you're selling. I just did a search on Popsike for The Eagles Hotel California LP. I found that 3473 have been sold since 2003. The prices range from $14 to $2211 in 2016 for a test pressing signed by 5 band members. Popsike prices are all over the place for most records. I only use it for very rare records. The Popsike website says they only archive records that sold for $20 or more, but have seen prices as low as $14.00.

Discogs is similar to eBay but is strictly for music. Vinyl records, cassettes, and CDs are listed for sale. There are millions of items for sale on Discogs. If you can't find it on eBay or Popsike, there's a good chance it will be for sale somewhere on Discogs.

Worthpoint.com.

Worthpoint has ten years of historical price data from all kinds of auction houses and sales sites. If you can't find any information from eBay, Amazon, or Google, you will most likely find it on Worthpoint. It's not free. It will cost you $23.99 a month, but you can get a 30-day free trial. During the trial you can do up to seven lookups before they start to charge for the service. I once had an item I could not find any information on, and I signed up for the free trial. I found the exact item and what it sold for. I waited a few days and cancelled the service.

Chapter 6

Getting Ready to List

Shipping Questions to Answer *Before* You Start
- Which shipping carrier will I use?
- Which shipping service?
- What are the shipping weight and package dimensions?

You'll put all this info into the listing form in the "Shipping details section".

Which shipping carrier will I use? The answer is the United States Postal Service (USPS), or Federal Express (FedEx). The shipping calculator will help you decide, and I talk about that later. About 95% of my packages are shipped with USPS.

Which shipping service? For the USPS you'll use Media Mail, First-class, Parcel Select or Priority. For FedEx it will be Ground/Home Delivery.

Media Mail is for items such as books, recorded media, and magazines without advertising. Check the USPS website to see what qualifies.

First-class is for items that weigh 16 ounces or less. Even though a DVD or CD will qualify for media mail, it is sometimes cheaper to ship first-class.

Parcel Select is for items that weigh over a pound.

Priority Mail is also for items that weigh over a pound. Priority Mail is considered an upgrade from Parcel Select. Priority Mail packages typically get to your customer faster. With the online shipping discounts, priority rates are usually within a few cents either way of Parcel Select. Another advantage with Priority Mail is that you can use the free priority shipping supplies from the post office.

Shipping weight and package dimensions: Shipping weight is the total weight including, box, packing material, label and tape. Package dimensions are the length, width, and height of the box after it is packed for shipping.

You need to know what box or package you intend to use *before* listing your item. Most boxes have the measurements on the bottom. Weigh your item. Add enough to cover the weight of the box, label and packing material. Weigh the box by itself or the box and item together. I keep a list of all the boxes I use regularly on my computer. I have the dimensions and weight right there so I can quickly look it up. I'll then add 3 ounces to the total weight to allow for packaging materials, tape etc. Always estimate on the high side to be safe. Say you add everything up, including the packing allowance and it comes to something like 1 pound, 15.9 ounces. That would make the shipping weight 2 pounds. But if it's that close I always go to the next highest one. The packing material is just an estimate. If your package weighs 2 pounds and half an ounce, you'll be charged for a 3 pound package.

Get Everything Together

Whatever you're listing, make sure it's ready to sell. Make sure the item is clean and not damaged. You don't want any price stickers anywhere. I'll wash glass items if they're dirty or dusty, which is often the case if you have picked up something at a yard sale. Be sure you have everything you need to do the listing, like a camera and a well-lit area for pictures. You'll want to have a tape measure close by to take measurements.

Taking Good Photos

eBay allows 12 photos per listing. I recommend using as many pictures as you can. Buyers want to see the product. Take a picture from every side including the top and bottom. Take close up pictures of anything the buyer needs to know about like any imperfections or damage. An example might be a vintage lunchbox. I would take at least six pictures of the outside: the top, bottom and four sides. Then take at least two or three pictures of the inside. If the thermos is included, I would take one inside picture with the thermos included, then two more with the thermos removed. Then you have three left for the thermos by itself. If there are scratches, damage or rust, take a close-up picture of that area. Sometimes I'll end up with more than twelve pictures. What I do then is go back and look at each one and decide what needs to stay and what I can eliminate. Sometimes you may need to go back and start over. This is one of the most important elements of the listing. Good, clear pictures can be the difference in *your* item selling instead of another seller.

Make sure the item is clean and ready to photograph. It's best to remove price stickers if you can do so without damaging the item. I use a Canon Powershot 12.1 MP digital camera. It's very easy to use and takes good close ups. An iPhone or other smartphone will work too, but I prefer to use a digital camera to take my pictures.

Take clear pictures. It's best to take your pictures in a well-lit area with a plain white background. This is the best way to show the true color of your product. Don't place the item on the floor or a crowded desk. Take an item you want to sell and do an eBay search. If you're on a computer, scroll down and check the "Sold Items" box. Look at the listings and the photos. Notice how other sellers present their items. Decide what you like and don't like. This is a good way to get ideas.

I use a simple white background for my photos. I use two pieces of white, 20" x 30" foam board that I got from the craft section at Wal-Mart. I have a work table in my office. Prop one piece up vertically against the wall or a box and lay the other one on the table and slide it right up against the vertical piece. For lighting, I use a pair of 20" LED table lamps with long, bendable necks placed on either side of the white foam boards. I sometimes place these on top of a stack of books to make sure the light source is well above the subject. Many sellers use photo booths for taking pictures. These are good for eliminating shadows and they distribute the light better. I don't use one because they're pretty bulky and I don't have a place where I want to leave a photo booth set up. I don't think they're necessary, but if you want to check them out, just do an eBay search for photo booth.

Don't be lazy with your pictures. Here's an example: Earlier this year I came across a seller that was selling vintage rock 8 track tapes. He had only *one picture* that showed an 8-track carry box full of tapes. He was listing all the tapes individually from that box using only the one picture. He had a listing with this title: "BOSTON 1976 Vintage 8 Track epic PEA 34188 Rock". The title is good, but I would have shown the tape by itself with a close up of the front label. There should have been pictures of the back, the opening showing the tape and pad and at least a couple of the edges.

Another example is a seller was complaining in an eBay group about getting negative feedback on a transaction. He was selling old cassette tapes in lots of 25 for craft purposes. I don't know what you would do with old cassette tapes, but there is a big market for craft items. There was only one picture of a huge box with hundreds of cassettes in it. Buying "one lot" meant you only get 25 cassettes. Even though the *description* was clear, the buyer thought he was getting everything in the picture. Don't risk it. Use as many pictures as you need to make sure the buyer understands what she's getting.

Getting Accurate Weights and Measurements

Unless I'm selling something like a DVD or a book, I want to put complete measurements in my listings. Put yourself in the buyer's shoes. What information would you like to have if you were buying this item? If I'm selling a vintage milk bottle, I'll tell the buyer how tall it is and the diameter across the bottom and the top.

When you're filling out the listing form, there's a place to enter package dimensions and weight. You need three box measurements: length, width, and height. Most boxes will have the measurements printed somewhere on the box, usually on the bottom. A box that says 10 x 8 x 6 on the bottom means that the box is 10" x 8" x 6" on the *inside*. The outside measurements are slightly larger. For this box you will need to enter measurements of 11 x 9 x 7 inches. I mentioned earlier that you need to know the packaged weight of your item before listing. This doesn't necessarily mean it needs to be packed ahead of time, just make sure you know what box you are going to use. Know the weight and the dimensions of the box. Weigh the flat box on your digital scale. If my scale says a box weighs 10.2 ounces, I round that up to 11 ounces. I have an excel file on my computer with a list of all the common boxes I use with the measurements and weights. I keep an inventory of several different sizes of plain corrugated boxes and priority mail boxes. When I'm getting ready to list an item, I have that information at my fingertips. It saves time.

Quick note about the sizes printed on boxes. Most all the plain corrugated boxes you buy will have the size printed on the bottom. These are the inside dimensions. The free priority mail boxes you get from the post office will usually have the size printed on the side. They show you both the inside and outside dimensions. No matter what box you use, though, you'll still measure it just before shipping.

Auction or Fixed Price?

As I mentioned before, when eBay first started, the only way you could sell was via auction. Today auctions comprise only about 10% to 15% of all eBay transactions. There are several reasons for this: Buyers today want to make an immediate purchase. There are so many users and so much competition that any item you list as an auction is probably available as Buy It Now. There may not be enough demand. Example: You have an item that you have researched and it has sold from $25 up to $50. There is one current "Buy it Now" listing with the item priced at $65.00. You paid $5.00 for it at a yard sale, so you list it at auction for 7 days and start the bidding at $1.00 with the idea of getting a lot of interest in it. You get a $1.00 bid the second day and then start to get a few watchers. Your item doesn't get any more bids and ends up selling for $1.00. This is not fun, but you are obligated to sell to the highest bidder. How do you avoid this happening to you? I'm glad you asked.

It depends on what you sell. There are very few items that I list as auction sales anymore. If you're selling more common items, then "Buy it Now" or "Fixed Price" is the only way to go. We'll cover pricing strategies in the next section, but if there are a lot of items listed, I will usually price my item somewhere in the middle unless I have purchased it really cheap and will make a good profit if it sells right away. I only list something at auction if it's rare and I know there's a demand for it, I've had it so long I just want to get rid of it, or I can't find any info at all. If I'm not sure what something will sell for, I start the auction at just enough to cover my fees.

Pricing Strategies

The price you decide on for your item depends on four things: What similar items have sold for, price range of active items, completed listings that ended *without* a sale, and demand for your item.

These strategies only apply to BIN, or fixed price listings. You should have already done some research before purchase, but you're going to do it again to make sure you price correctly. When deciding what price to list my item I look first at completed listings. This will show you all the listings that have ended, both sold and unsold. Look at the sold listings to see what your item has sold for. Look at completed, unsold listings to see the items that ended without selling. There are a lot of reasons why something doesn't sell: it was priced to high, there were too many listed, the listing is poorly done or the seller has poor feedback are some of the reasons.

After scanning completed listings, I scroll down and under the **Show Only** heading on the left I check the "Sold Listings" box. I usually look at the listings for the highest and lowest priced sold listings. The search results for sold listings will show the most recent listing first. If there are a lot of sold listings, use the drop - down menu at the top right to sort highest to lowest and lowest to highest price. When looking at the highest sold price, I try to determine why it sold higher. Did the seller write a better description? Was it in better condition than the others? Were there plenty of good pictures?

Now you know what items like yours *have actually sold for*. But you're not ready yet. You still need to check current listings. If a Tennessee Oilers Inaugural Season Coffee mug sold for $25.00 a few weeks ago and there are currently six of them listed for less than $10.00, there's a good chance that yours won't sell for $25.00.

Here's an example of how I might price a vintage 1967 Lost in Space dome lunch box: Say you scored this lunch box for $80.00 at an auction. It's in good condition with a few very minor scratches. It is complete with the thermos in good condition as well. Your on-site research shows that in the past 90 days these have sold from $80 to over $400 with most going for over $200.

What do you sell it for? There are 15 completed listings in the last 90 days, all sold. The lowest sold price is $80.95 for one that has a very visible scratch and no thermos. The highest sold price of $445.00 is a near mint example with a very nice thermos. There are two more that sold for $275 and $299 that included the thermos but were not in as good condition with minor nicks, rust etc.

Yours is in as good condition as the highest sold one, so let's look at the current listings before we list. There are eight for sale. Only two have the thermos. One thermos does not have the original cap and the lunch box has numerous scratches. The seller is asking $374.99. The other one has the right thermos and cap but shows a lot of rust inside. List price: $650.00. Based on what I see, I don't believe that either of those will sell for the listed price. But yours is in very similar condition to the one that sold for $445. I wouldn't think twice about pricing yours at $399.00 and expecting it to sell in a week or less. If you're in no hurry and are willing to wait a little longer, you might even put $450 or $475 on yours.

CHAPTER 7

LISTING YOUR ITEMS FOR SALE

You get 80 characters for the title; use as many of them as you can. Do not write the title in all caps or use special characters that don't mean anything like L@@K. A good title is about getting your listing to appear in search results. Words like L@@K, don't accomplish anything. Exclamation points also are not necessary. Capitalize the first letter of each word. It's not necessary to capitalize words such as like, and, to, or the. The eBay search engine looks for words that it believes are relevant to what the buyer is looking for. Always try to think like a buyer. Before I list, I always do an eBay search for the item. Look at the titles of the listings that appear at the top of the search listings. Try not to copy a title word for word, but look at it and try to get all the necessary information into your title.

TIP: Don't say "Like New" in your title. Buyers will often search using the keyword "new". In this case, your item may show up. This is also against eBay policy. Use the condition field and description for this.

Writing a Good Description

The first thing I like to do is restate my title in the first line of the description. I say something like "This listing is for _____", or "Up for auction is _____." Fill in the blank with the title of your listing. Then continue with the description. Point out the features and benefits. Clearly point out any flaws in your item. If you're selling a vintage collectible, it helps to include a sentence about how you acquired it. All these tactics make your listing stand out.

Do a search for your item. Read the descriptions in some of them to get ideas. Unless it's something like a DVD or CD, I like to add dimensions in the description. I see so many descriptions that say something like this: "In good condition, see photos." That's just lazy.

Here's a description I just copied from a vintage lunch box listing: "Up for consideration is a Vintage 1968 Chitty Chitty Bang Bang Metal Lunch Box that's in Excellent Condition. Looks all original showing signs of use including some slight dings, slight scratches, slight marring, not much paint loss and I don't see any broken or damaged parts. Looks quite clean inside (see photos 3-6). Wonderful graphics and color that would display nicely. Comes from my late father's collection of over 50 years"

Doesn't that sound better than: "Lunch box is in used condition. See pictures?"

Things NOT to put in your description: Don't say things like, "don't bid unless you intend to pay", "non-paying bidders will be reported to eBay", or "if you have less than X feedback ratings your sale will be cancelled". All this does is turn buyers off and such practice is discouraged by eBay.

Choosing the Right Category

Do a search for your item and check the top sold listing. Right below the eBay search bar you'll see the category this item was listed in. When you click on "sell one like this", or "sell similar item", the category will already be selected. You'll see a link which allows you to change the category if you wish.

The Easy Way to List *Anything*

Do an eBay search. For example, here's something I have on eBay now: "Vintage Pyrex Constellation Atomic Starburst Yellow." Look at the search results and pick one you like. Click on that listing. Under the pictures at the top you'll see: "$ Have one to sell?"followed by a link that says "Sell Now". When you click that link your selling form will load with the correct category and item specifics already selected. Just change the title a little and double check the item specifics before continuing to list. I cover the listing form later in this chapter.

The Easiest Items to List and Ship

The easiest items to list and ship on eBay are books, DVDs and CDs. Most of these could be shipped in a padded mailer. Your book description would mainly concern condition because the item specifics would load automatically.

To list these items simply type the bar code number into the search bar and hit search. Every bar code will have the corresponding numbers below it. Type in all the numbers you see, including the ones to the far left and far right, without any spaces. This way you are searching for EXACTLY that item, not something similar. Look at the search results, pick one and click on it. Below the main picture it says "Have one to sell?" with a link that says *"Sell now"*. You need to be logged in to your eBay account, but when you click that link, the "Create your listing" form will load with many of the details already filled in. The title from the original listing will be there. I recommend editing the title. The item specifics should also be filled in already. Just look at them to make sure it's right. The category is already selected and 99% of the time it will be right. Take a quick look at everything. DVDs, CDs, and books will usually be listed with the stock photo from eBay's catalog. If you're selling a new item, that's okay. I personally like to take my own pictures as I think the buyer wants to see what they're getting. I usually take at least a picture of the front and back.

You can actually use this method for anything that has a barcode. Experiment with other things if you like.

For example, I have a DVD set of Criminal Minds Season 13 in front of me. I bought it new and watched it once. If I were going to list it on eBay I would type in the barcode – 032429307972. My search shows prices from $27.99 pre-owned (free ship) to $50.81 new (2.85 shipping). Sold prices are from $12.99 to $42.47. I wouldn't put the barcode or condition in the title like some sellers do. There is a place for all that in the item specifics. For a title, I would put something like: "Criminal Minds Season 13 Three DVD Set Joe Mantegna /Matthew Gray Gubler". Don't worry about punctuation because you're not writing a sentence(be sure spaces are in the right place).The purpose of the title is to get your listing to show up in a search.

For the description, I would copy and paste the title. Otherwise, you don't need a long, detailed description. I would say something like, *"I bought this set new and watched it once. The discs are in pristine, like new condition."*

Listing Several of the Same Type of Items

If you buy a large quantity of the same type of items, it's easy to do a lot of listings if you do them all at once. An example is vinyl records. The only category you should use for vinyl albums is **Music > Records**. I recently bought a collection of about 60 LPs. I take pictures of ten at a time and list those. I'll start with a search for one like I'm listing, then click on "sell one like this". As with every type of item you sell, there are certain things that record buyers want to know, such as the vinyl grade, etc. But after I've listed the first record I'll just click on the "sell a similar item" button and keep going till I have ten done. You just need to change the title, pictures, update all the item specifics, price and description. If you're not using the global shipping program, you'll need to uncheck that box. It's usually already checked by default.

The Create Your Listing Form

There are several ways to get to this form. I'm starting as though you're already logged in and the listing form is ready.

There are four main sections on the listing form: listing details, selling details, shipping details, and sell it faster. Required entries have a red asterisk next to them.

Listing Details

Title

The most important part of the listing is the title. You must get this right. I talked about this in the first section of this chapter.

Right below the title field is a check box beside the text: "*Stand out with a bold title in search results ($4.00).*" I don't use this. It does exactly what it says. Your title is bold in the search results. I could never justify paying $4.00 for this.

Subtitle

I very rarely use this. The subtitle is a listing upgrade and will cost you $1.50. Then every time your listing is renewed, automatically or manually, you'll pay the $1.50 again. I have occasionally used this on a high-priced item, but only if I had important information I couldn't fit into the title. Shoppers can see the sub-title below the title in the search results.

Custom label

This is for your record keeping. It makes it easy to locate an item after it has sold. This is only necessary if you have a very large inventory of items listed. Set up your own storage and labeling system any way that makes sense to you. Just put the location code for the item in the custom label field as you're listing. When your item sells, whatever you put in this field will be in the sales record.

Category

When you get to the listing form via "sell similar", or "sell one like this", the correct category will already be selected. You can either use that category or change it to a different category. Click on "Change category" and you have a choice of recently used categories, search categories, or browse categories.

Second category

You can have your item show up in two different categories to increase chances of being found by buyers who search by category. For example, you may want to list an autographed Stephen King novel in "**Books > Fiction and Literature**" and

"**Collectibles > Autographs > Celebrities**". There is an extra fee for listing in a second category. For me it's 25 cents.

Store categories

This won't be visible unless you have a store subscription. You set up store categories based on what kinds of items you're selling. An eBay store gives you your own web address. Your store website includes your eBay user ID. Mine is https://stores.eBay.com/flatbed-ford. If you sell books, DVDs, and LP records, you might have a category for all three. You can have up to 300 store categories. To set up store categories, from your seller hub, scroll down to selling tools and click "Manage Store". In the upper left under Store Management you'll click "Store Categories."

Condition

This is a drop-down menu. The available selections are based on what you're selling. In most collectibles categories you can only select new or used.

Condition description

Anything you put in this box will appear right below the title in your listing. This is a very good place to call attention to something the buyer needs to know, like a flaw they should be aware of.

Photos

When you list an item for sale on eBay, you have to include at least one picture. The first picture you add, called the gallery photo, appears next to your item's title in search results and is the main photo in your listing. You can add up to 12 pictures. I don't do any editing on my pictures until I have uploaded them into the listing. Once the photos are in the listing, I use eBay's photo editor to do all my editing. The editor is right below the large picture. Click on any photo to edit it. Scroll over the icons to see what each one does. I almost always crop each photo (icon to the left) and auto adjust (magic wand icon to the right). Sometimes the auto adjust will make a big difference in how your pictures look. Right below the picture editor is a check box that says: *"Display a large photo in search results with Gallery Plus (fees may apply)."* I always check this box if I'm selling something in the antiques or collectibles categories because it's free for those categories. For other categories you'll pay 35 cents to 70 cents extra.

Item Specifics

This space is for details that are specific to your listing. Buyers can narrow search results based on what you put in here. Having as many item details as you can will improve your search rankings and allow the listing to more easily be indexed in Google. It takes a little practice to learn how to use item specifics correctly. Look at some of the highest priced sold listings and what item specifics they use.

Item description

This space is all yours. This is where you describe your item and let the buyer know why they should buy it. I talked about writing a good description in chapter 7, so I won't repeat it here.

Selling Details
Format

You'll see a drop-down menu that lets you select either auction style or fixed price.

Duration

The only option available in fixed price is Good 'Til Cancelled. These listings automatically renew every month, not every 30 days. They will relist each month on the same day you originally listed them unless you cancel the listing.

Under auction style you have the choice of 1, 3, 5, 7, or 10 days. You'll pay an extra fee of $1.00 per listing if you list an auction for 1 or 3 days.

Below duration you can decide when to start your listings. "*Start my listings when I submit them*" is selected by default. You can check "*Schedule to start on*", and fill in a starting time in the future. As you can see, there is a fee of ten cents to schedule an auction. I very rarely use this and then I will only use it for an auction style listing to schedule it to start in the evening.

Price

Fill in your selling price here for fixed price listings or your starting price for auction listings. Below the price field you can check this box if you want to allow buyers to make an offer on your item. This is available for fixed price or auction listings.

Quantity

This is the number of identical items in this listing. It will usually be one. If you are selling, for example, 5 identical copies of a CD, put 5 in this box. Each time one sells, the listing remains active and the quantity is reduced by the number sold. If a buyer wants two, they will enter 2 in the quantity field on the listing page. Listings with a quantity of more than one still only count as one listing in your free listings for the month.

Below the quantity field is a tick box called *"sell as lot"*. I've never used this, and I don't understand what it does. I've experimented with this setting and it didn't affect my listings. If you're selling items in a lot, just describe them that way in your listing.

Private Listing

Check this box if you don't want to reveal buyer's or bidder's identities.

Payment Options

The only thing you need to do here is check the box for PayPal payments unless you're using eBay managed payments.

Sales tax

You don't need to do anything here. eBay automatically collects sales tax from the buyer as I mentioned earlier.

Return options

Check *"domestic returns accepted"* if you accept returns. If you accept returns you will select 14, 30, or 60 days from the drop-down menu. In some categories you will only be able to choose 30 or 60 days. Then you'll choose free returns or buyer pays for returns. I have never checked replacement or exchange available. The last item is to check the box if you accept international returns. I've never checked this. I don't ship internationally so I don't use this.

Shipping Details

Domestic shipping

Select your shipping option. Flat rate, calculated shipping, freight, or local pick up.

I don't check the APO rate table box.

Select your shipping service from the drop-down menu. The shipping calculator is also available right above the menu.

Next you can check this box to offer another service. For example, you could offer both priority mail and FedEx, and the customer could choose their preference at check-out.

If your item is local pick-up only, you would select that in the shipping options drop-down. Check the *"offer local pick up"* box if you want to offer local pick in addition to shipping.

Under handling time select the number of business days you promise to ship by after a sale. This is what eBay uses to estimate delivery times. To get the Top-Rated discount you must offer same day or one day handling time. If you select same day you will see a link to set your shipping cut off time for same day shipping.

Combined shipping discounts: These are advanced shipping discounts that you set up in your shipping preferences.

International shipping

Check the *"sell internationally"* box to make your item available for the global shipping program.

Package weight and dimensions

I always select "package or thick envelope". There's no reason to choose anything else. Enter the box dimensions and package weight. I never check "irregular package".

Exclude shipping location

Here you can create a list of areas to exclude from this item. For example, you may want to exclude Alaska and Hawaii for a large, bulky or fragile item.

Item location

The town you're shipping from.

Sell It Faster

Promoted listings

Here you see a check box followed by: "*Boost your item's visibility with premium placements on eBay and pay only if your item sells!*" Then there's a link you can follow to learn more about it. Below that is a box that lets you set an ad rate and the amount you pay if the item sells via promoted listings. This means that you're **paying eBay to advertise your listing**. It may rank higher in the search results or it will be shown on another listing as a similar item. I believe that promoted listings also show up faster in a Google search. The amount you pay is a percentage of the sale price of the *item only*, not including shipping. You only pay the ad fee if someone buys the item as a result seeing the ad. The fee does not apply if your item is found through a normal search. I promote all my listings at one percent. eBay shows you the market rate. That's what eBay wants you to pay. I noticed a significant increase in my sales when I started promoting everything at one percent.

Volume Pricing

This works in conjunction with multiple quantity listings. If you have multiples you can give buyers a discount if they buy 2, 3, 4 or more of the same items.

At the very bottom of the listing form you see the listing fees you'll pay for this listing. If you are within you free listings for the month the fee amount will show $0.00. If you've added listing upgrades your extra fees will display here. Always check this before you hit the **List item** button at the bottom.

Chapter 8

Packing and Shipping

Your eBay item sold! You've worked hard to get to this point. There's nothing like the feeling when you get that email with the subject, "Your eBay Item Sold", or hearing the cash register "cha-ching" sound from the eBay app on your phone when something sells.

I get a lot of comments about how quickly packages arrive and how well they're packed. I almost always use new boxes, but I *will* pack something in a used box if it's in good shape. I typically wrap everything in bubble wrap. How much I use depends on how fragile the item is. I use masking tape to tape down the edge of the bubble wrap. This makes it easy for the customer to see where the tape is and makes it much easier to unwrap. I use a box big enough so the item can "float" in packing peanuts. There should be two inches of packing all the way around. YouTube has how-to videos that will teach you how to pack just about anything. It would take a really long book to cover all of them.

Here's a tip: Tape **all** the edge openings, not just the center seams. This will make your packages *six times* stronger. My customers rarely receive damaged boxes. Take some extra time and make your packages stand out from everybody else.

Packing Material

At the very least you need boxes, bubble wrap, packing peanuts or another type of filler, packing tape, and shipping labels. This is part of your cost of doing business. You can get all these items, with the possible exception of packing peanuts, at Wal-Mart, Office Depot, Dollar Tree, the UPS Store, and your local post office. Wal-Mart has a selection of several different sizes of boxes very cheap. Keep records of everything. I know that my cost to package an item is going to average around $2.00. Of course, if you only sell collectible stamps, yours will be different. Here is what I keep on hand:

Plain Boxes

I keep a quantity of various sizes of plain cardboard shipping boxes on hand. I get these from Uline Shipping Supply: uline.com. You have to buy a quantity of at least 25 at a time. I live in Middle Tennessee. Uline has a distribution warehouse near Atlanta, Ga. so if I need something fast, I can order right up to around 4pm and get them the next day. I also get boxes from Wal-Mart, the UPS Store and eBay. The UPS store has several sizes of multi-depth boxes that are great for shipping larger items.

Tip: I try to spend no more than an average of $1.00 per box for the majority of my items. The shipping cost from Uline is usually more than the cost of the boxes, but I try to make it average out to around a dollar per box. Wal-Mart has several sizes of boxes for less than a dollar. If you just need one or two boxes, check them out. No need to buy 25 of one size box if you don't have to.

Priority Mail Boxes

Priority mail boxes and padded envelopes are free from the United States Postal Service. You can pick up small quantities at the post office. You can also order online from the USPS in quantities of 10 or 25 each. I have an account with the USPS and order priority mail shipping containers from them. Any priority shipping supplies you order from the USPS are free, and they are shipped to you free. Here is a list of priority mail shipping stuff I like to keep on hand.

- Priority mail box 7 - 12x12x8 (this is not a flat rate box)
- Priority mail box 4 - 7x7x6 (not flat rate)
- Small flat rate box
- Medium flat rate box
- Large flat rate box
- Padded flat rate envelope
- Regular flat rate envelope
- Priority mail tape

These materials may only be used to ship priority mail shipments, and you pay whatever the current USPS rate is for that particular box.

Other shipping supplies: (Tape, bubble wrap, shipping labels, packing peanuts)

I usually get my tape and shipping labels at Wal-Mart. I use the Avery 18126 labels that come 10 sheets per pack, 20 labels per pack. Many sellers print shipping labels on plain white paper, cut the label as needed, and tape it to the box with clear tape. I also get bubble wrap at Wal-Mart. I use the large rolls that are around $17.00 plus tax.

I get packing peanuts from my local UPS store. I get the large 20 cubic foot bag which is about $32.00 plus tax. You can also get this on eBay for about the same price shipped.

eBayshippingsupplies

This is eBay's own shipping supplies seller. You can get everything you need at very reasonable prices. If you have a store subscription of at least a basic store or higher, you get a coupon each quarter to use in the eBay shipping supplies store. The coupons start at $25.00 for a basic store and go up based on your store subscription. The user ID is ebayshippingsupplies.

Get shipping supplies cheap (or free): Here some ways to save money on your shipping supplies:

- Get packing materials from work or stuff that is thrown away.
- Use free priority mail supplies when possible
- Buy paper for shipping labels at sales like yard sales or estate sales.
- Use the smallest box you can get by with to safely pack your item.

Be sure you have proper shipping supplies before listing anything. I once bought a pick-up truck load of 1940s wallpaper at an auction. It was a hardware store that had been there since the 1920s and had been closed for several years. The store, located in Dickson, TN was called Nick's Hardware. Nick's was actually featured in an episode of American Pickers. I got all that wallpaper for $80.00 for the whole lot, but I had a lot of work to do before listing. Some of the rolls had some water damage and I went through every single roll, pulling some off and cutting off the damage. I went to Uline.com and bought heavy cardboard tubes for shipping. I happened to have some plastic bags on hand that worked well to wrap the rolls in. There was a lot of work involved, but there were a couple of hundred rolls that I eventually sold for $25 to $30 a roll.

Calculated Shipping or Flat Rate Shipping?

This one is easy. If you choose free shipping, media mail, or something you know is going to qualify for a priority mail flat rate box, choose flat rate shipping. Everything else is calculated shipping. Not long ago, I would have included first-class shipping in the flat rate category, but with a recent post office rate change, first class shipping prices are now based on distance as well as weight.

Which Carrier Should I Use?

I only use USPS or FedEx. In the past I would use UPS for larger packages or items too expensive for the postal service. Now I use USPS Parcel Select or FedEx for larger packages. This is a personal preference for me. Using UPS means you must set up a UPS shipping account to get the eBay shipping rates. When you pay for the label the amount comes out of your PayPal account immediately, but there is something else going on. PayPal is just putting a hold on those funds for a few days until they get the final bill. Then PayPal will *return* that money to your account. A few days later they deduct it again. You just need to remember this. I once thought I had plenty of money in my account to cover my shipping for the day and logged in to see something different. The money was taken out, then put back and I forget to keep up with it.

The size of the box is usually what determines whether I ship

FedEx or USPS. The post office has used dimensional weight to determine shipping costs for a while, but in June 2019 they reduced the size of the box to determine what qualifies for dimensional ship rates. The shipping rate for a box that measures more than one cubic foot on the outside is calculated using dimensional weight and actual weight. Then the higher of the two is used for the shipping rate. One cubic foot is 12" x 12" x 12". If the length, width and height added together measures more than 36 inches, it may be cheaper to go FedEx, as their rates are much cheaper than USPS for larger items.

Here's an example of shipping rates for a five pound package measuring 16 x 12 x 8 inches shipped from my home town to Chicago:

- USPS $9.12
- FedEx $13.50

Notice the box measurements total 36". If you add **one inch** to *any measurement,* look what happens to the shipping cost.

- USPS $15.93
- FedEx $13.59

This example is based on rates in effect November 2019.

A couple of things to keep in mind with FedEx: You should be sure you have a place nearby to drop off packages. There's not a FedEx store near my house, but I can drop them at Office Depot. Also, when you print your label, you don't pay for it immediately. FedEx bills eBay once a month and eBay adds it to your invoice for the following month.

Tip: When you're just starting out, try to stay with things you can ship USPS and will fit in a box measuring less than a cubic foot.

Free Shipping or Not?

Some sellers don't use free shipping at all. Some use it exclusively and some mix it up. I'm not against using free shipping but I don't use it that much. There are arguments that say having free shipping on your listing moves it higher in the search results, but I've never noticed a difference. There is one advantage, though. In the search results an item will stand out because it says "Fast 'N Free" next to your listing.

The only time I use free shipping is when I know what the shipping cost is, and I can build that into the price of my item.

Which Shipping Service Should I Use?

If you use FedEx, always ship Ground or Home Delivery. The following rules apply to the postal service. This is intended only as a guide, but these rules will usually apply.

5 ounces or less: First class mail. Even items that qualify for the media mail rate will probably ship for less with first class.

Over 5 ounces up to 16 ounces: Ship it first class unless it qualifies for media mail.

Over a pound but not more than 5 pounds: These will ship Parcel Select or Priority Mail. Nine times out of ten I'll ship priority instead of parcel select. It's actually cheaper for me because of the discounts I get as a Top-Rated seller. Priority is an upgrade for the customer and usually will arrive sooner.

Over 5 pounds: Use the shipping calculator to determine the best way to ship.

How to Use the Shipping Calculator

The eBay shipping calculator is your best friend. You can find it here: https://www.eBay.com/shp/Calculator. If the link doesn't work by clicking on it, or if you're reading the paperback version, log in to your account and type it in manually. Any time I publish a link I always check to make sure it works. For some reason this one didn't. But when I manually type it as it is here, it worked fine. The eBay shipping calculator is also available from inside the listing form. You need the *outside* box measurements and the shipping weight for the calculator.

This is how I use the calculator to determine shipping method. First, enter the package type in the menu at the top. Always select "Package". Enter the box dimensions and weight. If the *shipping weight* is 15 ounces or less, round up to the next ounce and enter that into the ounces box. Remember that this is the total shipping weight including packing material. Anything over a pound you'll round up to the next pound and enter only the pounds into the Lbs. field. Enter your zip code and hit enter.

Next you see a page that shows your shipping costs to three different locations. By default, you're shown all the USPS services that qualify for this shipment. You can see the online costs as well as paid in store rates. You can then select FedEx (or UPS if you wish) to see what the shipping costs are for those. By comparing these numbers, you should know how you're going to ship the item.

What to Do When an Item Sells

When an item sells, you're notified by email. In addition to emails, you will also get a notification on your my eBay page, or your seller hub. If you have the mobile app, when you open the app, you will see the notification right on the home page.

When I log into my seller hub, I see the orders right there in the tasks section. If the order is already paid, there is a link called "Print labels and ship". If the order needs to ship today there will also be a link that says "Ship within 24 hours". If a sale has not been paid for it will say "Awaiting payment."

Clicking the "print labels and ship" link takes you to the "Manage orders awaiting shipment page". If the order has been paid for, there is a link to print the shipping label. Clicking this link takes you to the shipping label page. Here you fill out all the details to pay for and print your label.

On the left you see your order details. In the large window to the right are all the delivery details with selections already made based on how you set up the listing. Under "Service" you'll see two or three options with the "Buyer selected" link already highlighted. I'm looking at one of mine right now that has three options: Parcel select for $7.89, priority mail package for $7.76 and priority mail express for $26.65. The buyer paid for parcel select, but in this case, I'll select priority package. The cost is a few cents less for me but a shipping upgrade for the customer.

At the top left you see a link where you can edit the shipping address if the buyer has requested it. At the top right you'll see a drop-down menu called "Ship on". This is the day you need get the package to the post office.

At the bottom you'll notice a few other things. Here is where you add insurance, add a custom note to the buyer in the shipping confirmation email, and a check box to require a signature for delivery.

Shipping Questions Answered

Shipping, I believe, is the most confusing area for new sellers, and most of the questions I see in the eBay help groups deal with shipping.

Here's a list of some of the questions I see asked over and over in the Facebook groups.

Do I have to use priority mail boxes for priority shipping? No. You can use any box. You can't go the other way. If you use any of the free priority shipping containers or tape, you must pay for priority postage.

How do I add tracking information to another item shipped in the same package? This is the same as combining more than one item into one shipment. There's a way to do this in the advanced settings, but here is a simpler way: I just shipped a package yesterday where I did this. I had listings with multiples of two different 1976 vintage key chains. Both key chains were similar themes. A buyer bought and paid for one, then bought and paid for the other a couple of hours later. It was two separate transactions. I had the listings set up as free shipping because the total packaged weight is less than two ounces. I put both items into one package (the total weight still under two ounces, which saved me money on shipping). I printed out the shipping label as usual and sealed the package. In the seller hub go, to the "Orders" drop-down menu and select "paid and shipped". The item you just printed the label for will be at the top. Click on the tracking number. This brings up the tracking details where you can select and copy the tracking number. Then go back to your "manage orders awaiting shipment". There's a link there that says "add tracking". It's a light gray text that doesn't look like a clickable link but it is. On the next page just copy in the tracking number and fill in the carrier and click save. You have combined two orders into one package.

How does the Global Shipping Program work? This program allows you to offer worldwide shipping while letting eBay handle all the details. When you fill in your shipping details there is a box you can check if you want to make your listing available for the service. When an international buyer purchases, all you have to do is print your label the same as any other. Your label will print out the address to the global shipping center in Kentucky. You only pay to ship to Kentucky. Your buyer will see the total shipping cost which *includes* shipping to the global shipping center and shipping to their international address.

What if I have set up my listing as priority shipping but it costs me more to ship than what the buyer paid? Can I use a cheaper option? No. The buyer may have purchased specifically because it had priority shipping. In this case you will just have to eat the difference.

Should I refund extra shipping charges to the customer? If it's only a couple of dollars I wouldn't worry about it. I will usually refund some of the shipping cost if it's over by $5.00 or more.

How do I get the commercial shipping discounts on eBay? According to what's on eBay's website as of April, 2020, you get *Commercial Base* shipping rates when buying and shipping your labels through eBay. I don't know what the current discount is for commercial base. Commercial Plus pricing, however, gives you a significant discount over buying your shipping at the post office. To get the commercial plus pricing you must be a Top-Rated seller or ship 300 packages a year.

While you can't take advantage of the Commercial Plus rates when you're a new seller, there may be other option. It's called Pirate Ship.

Should I use a third-party shipping service like stamps.com or Pirate ship? I don't use any of those, but a lot of sellers like Pirate Ship. I've checked out Pirate Ship rates and have found they they're not any better for me. If you're just getting started, you should check them out. You can get the same shipping rates with Pirate Ship as you would with commercial plus Top-Rated seller rates. Check it out at pirateship.com.

How do I void a shipping label? For example, if you've entered the weight wrong or selected media mail when it should be priority, you'll need to void the label if it's already been paid for. But you should print another label first. In your seller hub under the "Orders" tab click on the shipping labels link. You'll see a list of recent shipping labels. Under "more actions", select "print another label". Then a form will come up and you can put in the correct information. You WILL have to pay for the label again. Then go back to the original label and click void and answer the questions. It will usually take a couple of weeks to get a refund for the voided label, because the post office needs to make sure it has not been used.

I printed a prepaid label at home. Do I need to wait in line at the post office for a receipt? Most post offices have an area where you can just leave packages without having to wait. If you have a large quantity of packages it may not be practical to wait in line. I don't need the receipt, but I like to see my packages scanned in. I've had a few times where a package was set aside at the end of the day and it sat at the post office for several days before leaving. I once sold a vintage magazine to a customer in Nashville, TN (40 miles from me). The purchase was Friday and he needed it Saturday as a gift for a friend's birthday party. I had hundreds of vintage Scientific American magazines listed. These do not qualify for media mail so I had the listings set up to ship priority mail. The books fit nicely in a flat rate priority mail envelope (enclosed in a magazine bag, of course). There were several identical copies of this magazine listed, but he bought mine because the listing guaranteed delivery the next day. He contacted me Monday after the mail ran and still had not received it. The customer was not happy. The package sat in my home post office until Tuesday before it finally began its journey. My customer understood when I explained what happened. Even though it was not my fault, I refunded the entire purchase.

Do I need insurance? I only buy extra insurance for items worth $250 or more. You can add it when you buy the shipping label if you wish. Priority mail includes $50.00 of insurance at no extra cost. If you're shipping an expensive item it's a good idea to get insurance. You can't charge buyers for insurance in your listing, but you can build it into the cost of your item. If you do have a damage claim, *you* will need to file the claim, not the buyer.

When should I have the customer sign for the package? When you print labels through eBay, tracking is included at no cost. If I have an item that sells for $250.00 or more, I require a signature on delivery. When you're filling out the label information, there's a box you can check if you want to require a signature. Just make sure that somewhere in the listing description you mention it so the buyer is aware of it.

A customer says they didn't receive the item but my tracking shows delivered. This is not your responsibility. If you've shipped to the address the customer has on file, then you've done your job. The customer has the same tracking information you have. They should make an effort to see where it is. I once had a customer find a package a few days after tracking showed it delivered. The mailman couldn't get to the house and left it the back of a pick-up. I once had a package that showed delivered to me but I could not find it anywhere. I went to the post office and asked them to help me locate it. Their GPS tracking showed it had been scanned as delivered two houses down from mine. I went down to that house and retrieved my package.

Covid-19 update

Since April 2020, USPS packages all over the country are delayed. Shipping volume has increased so much that the post office doesn't have the delivery capability to keep up. There are a lot of complaints about late shipments. Sellers are getting dinged for late delivery even though it's out of our control. Just make sure you ship on time. I've actually changed all my handling times to two business days. I still ship next day or sometimes the same day, but this gives me a cushion so my packages arrive when they're expected.

You still need to specify next day or same shipping to get top-rated seller discounts, but I'll sacrifice that for now. You can contact eBay and they'll remove any defects for late delivery during the pandemic, but they're hard to get in touch with right now. I prefer to be proactive.

Remember, you can always adjust your handling time to fit your schedule. If you're going to be away for a long weekend and returning Monday, set your handling time for two business days in case you're not back in time to get shipments out.

Chapter 9

Opening an eBay Store

Having an eBay Store won't have a huge impact on your sales. It probably won't do much to bring you customers unless you work very hard to promote it. But depending on how many items you plan to list, having a store can save you a lot of money in fees.

As you read in chapter 2, eBay gives you 50 free listings each month without a store subscription. You'll pay .35 for each listing after you reach 50.

To be sure you have up to date information, check the eBay selling fees pages for the current rates. There are different sets of fees for selling with or without a store subscription.

You can choose a monthly subscription or a yearly subscription. It's cheaper to select the yearly subscription. You don't have to pay a year in advance, but you *are* agreeing to keep the subscription for a year when you choose the yearly option. If you cancel before the year is up, you're charged an early termination fee of one-third of the balance remaining on your subscription.

Here's a simple way to decide if you need an eBay store subscription:

A **Starter** store will save you money if you plan to have 75 or more listings per month. A starter store is $4.95 a month for a yearly subscription or $7.95 a month for a monthly subscription.

A **Basic** store will save you money if you plan to have 175 or more listings per month. A basic store is $21.95 a month for a yearly subscription or $27.95 a month for a monthly subscription.

There are three store levels above the basic level. They are **Premium**, **Anchor**, and **Enterprise**. If you're selling enough to have a premium store, you're no longer a beginner, and probably don't need this book.

Another advantage to having a store is that the final value fees for all store levels except the starter store are lower. For example, listings in the collectibles and music/records categories are 10% for a basic store or a starter store and 9.15% for all the other subscriptions.

There are other advantages to having a store subscription. The one I like is the shipping supplies coupon. I talked a little about this earlier. Basic stores and above get a quarterly coupon to use in the eBay shipping supplies store. The coupon is $25.00 for basic stores, $50.00 for premium stores, and $100.00 for anchor stores. The user ID for the shipping supply store is ebayshippingsupplies.

Having a store also allows to you create discounts and sales. You can create a sale for one item or a whole category. The sale will run for as long as you choose, and eBay makes a link available where buyers can see everything you have on sale.

Having a store allows you to put your store in vacation mode. Turning vacation mode on only displays a notice at the top of your listings that you are away and won't be able to ship until the date you specify. Buyers can still purchase your items. It's a good idea to increase your handling time to make sure you don't have any late shipments. If you plan to be away for several days or a week or so, my advice is to just go ahead and end all your listings until you are ready to ship again.

Chapter 10

Seller Performance Standards

Top-Rated means you're one of the best sellers on eBay, providing an exceptional quality of customer service as well as meeting minimum sales requirements for the Top-Rated Seller level. If you're a Top-Rated Seller, you're also eligible for the Top-Rated Plus listing benefits as long as you meet the listing qualifications.

Above standard: You're meeting the minimum standard for sellers and doing a good job of looking after your customers.

Below standard: You're not meeting one or more of the minimum requirements for customer service quality.

Becoming a Top-Rated Seller

Back in the day, eBay shoppers would see prominent "PowerSeller" logos at the tops of certain auctions and fixed priced listings, indicating that the seller in question was among eBay's best and most experienced. When the Top-Rated Seller program emerged the powerseller logos disappeared from the listings.

In eBay's seller performance standards article, they still list the qualifications to become a powerseller, even though, to my knowledge, they no longer support that program.

Becoming a Top-Rated Seller indicates that you consistently deliver outstanding customer service; it also makes you eligible to receive a prominent Top-Rated Plus seal on qualifying listings. To be a Top-Rated seller you need to:

- Have an eBay account that's active for 90 days
- Have at least 100 transactions and $1,000 in sales with US buyers over the past 12 months
- Meet the requirements for transaction defect rate, cases closed without seller resolution, and late shipment rate

When you become a Top-Rated seller, you **are eligible** to have the Top-Rated plus seal prominently displayed at the top of your listings.

Top-Rated Plus Benefits and Requirements

As a Top-Rated Seller, you can qualify for exclusive Top-Rated Plus benefits if you offer same or 1-business-day handling time and 30-day or longer free returns. Yes, you read that right. You must agree to ship your item on the same or next business day and offer at least 30 days for the buyer to return the item. You must also offer free returns, meaning you cover the cost of the return. You can still be a Top-Rated seller without offering free returns, but the buyer won't see the Top-Rated plus seal unless your listing offers 30 day or longer free returns.

You also get a 10% discount on final value fees for Top-Rated plus listings. On most of my listings, I have 30-day free returns to get the Top-Rated plus seal at the top. But there are some items that I don't list with free returns. In a nutshell, I don't use the free return option if I'm selling something over $100. I'll cover returns in more detail in the next chapter.

Chapter 11

Managing Your eBay Business

Here's an actual email from a buyer to a seller in one of the Facebook groups I'm in. The buyer opened an item not as described case (INAD) for this item.

"I want to return this cat food dish. It's defective. My cat won't eat out of it."

Returns

Returns can be confusing. The following paragraph is taken from an article on the eBay site: Setting up your return policy.

"When you sell on eBay, you need to state whether you accept returns or not, and if so, under what conditions. For example, you might assert who pays for return shipping or that you're willing to accept returns for a specific period of time after a sale. Whatever you decide your policy is, it needs to be clearly specified in your listings."

Here are some of the reasons a buyer may want to return an item:

- They don't like it or changed their mind.
- The item is damaged.
- The wrong item was sent
- The item doesn't match the description.

When a buyer requests a return, you have the option of refunding the purchase price immediately, or waiting until the item is returned. I don't refund the buyer until I have the item back. If the return is due to buyer's remorse and the item is received back in original condition, refund the purchase price only, not the shipping cost. If it was free shipping, you will refund the entire amount.

Here are some things you can do to prevent returns:

- Limit selling frequently returned items like clothing and shoes.
- Use eBay's relatively new service "Authenticate First" – sometimes sellers are under the impression that they are selling genuine Gucci when in fact it is a knockoff. Take authenticity out of the game and buyers will have peace of mind knowing their product is 100% genuine.
- Make sure your items are exactly as described. Include all measurements and make the buyer is aware of any flaw. Don't say something is new if it is like new. If a box has been opened and you know the item is new and never used its okay to say *New in open box.*
- Make sure each and every item is properly working and that you have included all necessary parts. When running a large eBay business, people sometimes forget about quality assurance – don't!
- It is crucial to choose what items to sell wisely – for more complex items you should include clear instructions to prevent returns due to users not understanding how to use your product or not having the time to learn.

Package items very carefully especially if the item is fragile. Spending a little extra money on bubble wrap or packing paper (or free old newspapers and magazines) will save you headaches and return expenses in the long term!

When setting up your listing you can select "No returns" or "Seller accepts returns." In my opinion it's better to accept returns. You can select "Free returns", where you pay for return shipping, or "Buyer pays return shipping."Here are the ways you can set your return policy:

- No returns
- 14-day buyer-paid returns
- 14-day free returns
- 30-day buyer-paid returns
- 30-day free returns
- 60-day buyer-paid returns
- 60-day free returns

14-day returns are only available for these categories: Camera Drones, Camera Lenses, Collectibles & Art, Digital Cameras, Jewelry, and Medical & Mobility.

eBay *wants* you to offer free returns. You must offer 30-day or 60-day free returns to qualify for the top-rated plus benefits and the badge on your listings. When you allow free returns and a customer requests a return, eBay will automatically approve it and charge you for the return shipping. The customer prints a return label and the charge is added to your next invoice. There is another advantage to free returns. When the item is returned and it's found not to be in original condition, damaged or a different item is returned (*this does happen*), you can choose to refund only a portion of the purchase price or not at all. You always have the option to call eBay customer service and they'll help if you have a problem.

I personally use different policies based on what I'm selling. If an item is not expensive or very lightweight (not more than 2 pounds), I'll use free 30-day returns. If a customer requests a return, eBay automatically approves it and generates the return label. On most other items, I use 30-day buyer paid returns. In rare cases I might sell something defective which I clearly identify as *no returns – for parts or repair only.*

Trying to decide the best return policy will make your head spin, but it's not really a big deal. If you do everything right on the front end, your returns won't amount to enough to worry about.

In the case of the cat food dish above, the seller had free returns. Since the item was returned used and not in the same condition, the seller wasn't required to issue a refund. He was only out the cost of the return shipping.

Feedback

97% of online buyers read reviews before making a purchase.

Your eBay feedback is your customer service history. Every feedback you've ever received is recorded for the world to see (unless you choose to make your feedback private). Buyers can leave sellers a positive, negative, or neutral feedback rating for a transaction. The buyer can also leave detailed seller ratings in four areas: Description, shipping cost, shipping speed, and communication. Sellers can only leave positive feedback for buyers.

When a buyer leaves feedback, they're telling you how they feel about the transaction. Feedback comments should be professional and describe what you like or dislike without threatening or derogatory comments. If you are happy with a purchase you might say something like, *"My item was as described and shipped promptly"*. I take great care to package securely and I get a lot of comments about good packing and how fast the item was shipped.

Leaving feedback as a buyer

I ALWAYS leave feedback for every seller I buy from on eBay. I will very rarely leave neutral or negative feedback. I always give a seller an opportunity to resolve a problem. I don't remember leaving more than one negative feedback in all my years on eBay.

Leaving feedback as a seller

For many years, it has been my policy only to leave feedback for a buyer after they have left me positive feedback. There are a lot of different opinions on this and it's not for me to say what's right or wrong. This is just the way I do it. I've had a couple of transactions where I left positive feedback for a buyer and then they left me negative feedback.

You can set up your eBay preferences to automatically leave positive feedback with generic comments you choose. It can be set to automatically leave feedback as soon as the buyer pays or after the buyer leaves you positive feedback. I choose to leave feedback manually because I like to read the comments first.

What to do if a buyer leaves you a negative or neutral feedback

The first thing to do is take a deep breath. It's not the end of the world. I remember the first negative I ever received. I was pissed! But what I was most angry about is that the buyer did not contact me and let me have a chance to fix the problem. I'm very careful with my listing descriptions, pictures, packing and shipping. I have probably received no more than ten negative feedbacks in twenty plus years. All but a couple of them were because the buyer didn't read everything. The others were something I missed in the listing but the feedbacks were, in my opinion, unfair because I never got the chance to work it out.

I prefer the customer contact me right away if there's a problem so I have a chance to fix it.

Feedback extortion

When a buyer says something like, "give me a partial refund if you don't want negative feedback", or "how well you deal with this problem will determine what kind of feedback you get", that's called feedback extortion, and it's something eBay does not allow. The buyer can get suspended or even banned from eBay for this, and any negative feedback will be removed by eBay in this situation.

Negative feedback doesn't affect how eBay measures a seller's performance. For its part, eBay is more concerned with a seller's defect and late shipment rates and whether they have cases that were closed without resolution than the buyer reviews. For sellers, however, buyer ratings and feedback are very important, as they influence other buyer's decisions and can dissuade them from making a purchase.

The first step in getting negative feedback removed is to contact the buyer directly. The feedback can be revised, but only with a mutual agreement of both parties, at which point the seller can notify eBay that they're willing to have the feedback withdrawn.

To get the discussion going, sellers can reach out to a buyer by clicking on the "Help & Contact" link on eBay, selecting the item in question (which should be pictured), choosing "Contacting a buyer or bidder," and then clicking "Contact buyer."

That will take the seller to a page where they can write a note appealing directly to the buyer, explaining the situation. For instance, did the item ship late? A seller can explain why this happened and assure the buyer that it will not happen again. Or they can offer an explanation of whatever else led to the buyer's dissatisfaction.

Requesting Feedback Revision Through eBay

If a buyer is willing to revise feedback, the seller can request a feedback revision through eBay. A seller can make five such requests annually for every 1,000 ratings received, and the process is straightforward and simple.

Feedback Revision requests can be made by clicking the "Go to Feedback Forum" link on the "My eBay" page. Then select the "Request Feedback Revision" link in the right rail, choose the item in question and leave the revision details.

The buyer has 10 days to respond to the revision request from eBay, at which point they can agree to the revision and their original comments will no longer be visible; they can also deny the request and provide a reason to eBay, which may or may not be shared with the seller, depending on the buyer's preference; or they can simply ignore the request and not respond.

If the latter happens, the revision request will simply expire after 10 days and the feedback will remain. In this case, a seller does also have the option of responding to the feedback with a reply to the feedback detailing their version of events.

If for whatever reason a seller is unable to request a feedback revision but one is warranted, the buyer can also follow up with an additional comment, expounding on their original feedback.

Feedback can also be removed if the feedback in question is threatening, obscene, offensive, or presents a clear danger to the person about whom it was left. For instance, if a reviewer includes personal details about the seller in feedback such as a telephone number, address, or the person's full legal name, the feedback would be subject to removal. Even if the buyer has a valid concern, eBay would remove the review.

Customer Service

I define good customer service as:

- Describing my items accurately
- Shipping promptly and packaging professionally
- Handling customer questions and complaints professionally

Two words: Be nice. Don't take it personally. Buyers don't read everything. They make unreasonable requests. They don't look at all the pictures you've worked so hard to get right. I once had a vintage lunch box listing with twelve pictures. I got a message from a potential buyer asking if I could provide more pictures. I replied asking him if he needed pictures other than the twelve in the listing. Yes, I confess it wasn't exactly a professional response. He thought there was only one picture because he didn't take time to go through the whole listing. Try to be professional in your response. Also, remember that you don't have to respond to something absolutely ridiculous. If a buyer offers $10.00 for something you have listed for $50 with a story about why you should sell it for that, just ignore it and move on. There are better things you can do with your time. Here's a message I once got from an angry buyer and how I dealt with it.

I had my preferences set to automatically open an unpaid item case if I had not received payment within four days. A few years ago, two days before Thanksgiving, a buyer received an item she purchased via auction listing. Since it was an auction, she wasn't required to pay immediately. So, naturally when she didn't pay within four days, an unpaid item case automatically opened. What follows is her email to me – which was sent literally minutes after she was notified of the unpaid item case:

"I just received an email that an unpaid item case was opened against me for this item. I am very taken back. I will pay for the item this weekend, but given it has been just 4 days since the item closed, and it's a holiday week and I was traveling, as was most of the country, I am alarmed a seller would open a case so quickly, especially given the dynamics of it being a busy holiday the past few days. Very disappointed and upset at such behavior. I will pay for the item as I intended to and because it's the right thing to do, but I will not be purchasing again from you as a seller."

The buyer was obviously getting her emails. She went ahead and paid a few minutes after sending that email. She didn't have time to pay when eBay sent her the initial payment request. She didn't have time to pay when eBay sent a payment reminder a couple of days later. But she suddenly had time to send that message and pay for the purchase during the *busy Thanksgiving weekend*. It's only natural to want to fire back a response and *"tell them what you think"*. Don't do it. Don't respond right away. I immediately typed out a response that was not exactly professional. I didn't send it. I waited until the next morning and sent this reply:

"Good morning. Thank you for contacting me. Please accept my apologies for the misunderstanding. I have my eBay account set up to automatically open unpaid cases after 4 days. I set it up this way years ago. I used to put a sentence in all my listings stating that an unpaid item case would be opened automatically after 4 days. I don't do that anymore. All my listings, including this item, just say something like "please make payment within 3 days." What I do now is just send a message after 3 days asking the buyer if they need more time and then turn off the unpaid item assistant. But I just got home late last night from a family trip and it totally slipped my mind. I'm retired and I sell on eBay full time now. This is part of our income. Having an unhappy customer is the last thing I want. Any time a buyer has a problem with anything they buy from me, I go out of my way to take care of it immediately. My feedback speaks for itself. I'm going to change my settings so this doesn't happen again. Your item will ship tomorrow. If there is any problem at all with your purchase, please contact me right away."

What if the Buyer Doesn't Pay?

The best way to prevent having unpaid items is to avoid them in the first place. Set all your fixed price listings to *Immediate Payment Required*. Auction listings can't be set to require immediate payment. If you allow best offer, you can't collect payment immediately when you accept an offer.

I no longer set my preferences to automatically open an unpaid item case. eBay sends the payment invoice and payment reminder a few days later. If I don't receive payment on the fourth day, I send this message: *"Hello, just a reminder that I haven't received payment yet. If you need more time, please let me know. If for some reason you no longer want the item, let me know and I'll be happy to cancel the sale."* If I still don't get a response after two more days, I manually open an unpaid item case at that time. A customer will usually pay at this point. If they don't, you can close the case in a few more days and eBay will refund your final value fee.

Canceling a Sale or Ending a Listing

There will be cases when you need to cancel a sale or end listings. You can cancel a sale up to 30 days after it is sold. If the item is damaged or lost you can cancel the sale, but you risk getting a defect when cancelling for this reason. You may, however, cancel a sale without a defect if the buyer requests it. There are many reasons why a buyer may want to cancel. Whatever the reason, if you haven't shipped the item yet, it's better to go ahead and cancel.

You can end active listings anytime. If you have an auction listing running that already has bids, you must first cancel the bids.

I don't do this unless the item is damaged or lost. Buyers don't like it and eBay doesn't like it.

Defects and How to Avoid Them

Your eBay defect rate is the single most important metric you have to worry about as a seller. If it gets bad, you can expect search penalties, selling limitations, eBay Store downgrades, and even higher fees. Knowing how to keep yours as low as possible is one of the most important survival skills a seller can have.

What is a defect or defective transaction?

eBay states that there are three kinds of defects:

- Transactions canceled by the seller.
- eBay Money Back Guarantee cases where eBay decided in favor of the buyer.
- PayPal Purchase Protection cases where PayPal decided in favor of the buyer.

Seller-Canceled Transactions

This is perhaps the most common cause of defects for honest sellers. If you have to cancel the transaction for any reason—for example, if you run out of stock—it counts. (Problems that are completely the buyer's fault, like them failing to pay, don't count.)

eBay Money Back Guarantee Claims

The eBay Money Back Guarantee comes into play under either of two circumstances:

1. The item you sent to the buyer doesn't match your description.
2. The buyer doesn't receive the item.

The buyer also has to meet several conditions, including reporting the issue within a time limit (generally 30 days of receiving / not receiving the item) and contacting you first. You have plenty of chances to resolve the problem. But if you don't, and eBay decides in favor of the buyer as they usually do, it counts as a defect.

PayPal Purchase Protection Claims

PayPal Purchase Protection applies to the same situations as the eBay Money Back Guarantee when the item isn't received or isn't as described. However, PayPal has less demanding requirements for the buyer than eBay. They also have a deadline of 180 days rather than 30.

Just like with eBay, the buyer needs to reach out to you for resolution first. Settling with the buyer directly will allow you to avoid the risk of a defect.

What is the eBay Defect Rate?

Your eBay defect rate consists of the number of defects you've had (as described above) divided by your total transactions. If you had three defects after selling 100 items, your defect rate would be 3%.

Exactly when it affects your account depends on several conditions.

An important qualifier to note here is the "evaluation period" or "look back period".

- If you've sold <u>less than</u> 400 items in the last three months, your evaluation period is the last 12 months.
- If you've sold <u>at least</u> 400 items in the last three months,

your evaluation period *is* those three months.

Everything listed below is dependent on your evaluation period. If something happened before your current evaluation period began, it doesn't count.

A Top-Rated Seller will lose Top-Rated status if **either** of the following happens:

- Their defect rate is higher than 0.5%
- They have defects from at least three different buyers.

All sellers will be penalized for non-performance if **any** of the following happens:

- They have defects from at least four different buyers.
- Their defect rate is higher than 2%.
- At least two eBay Money Back Guarantee and/or PayPal Purchase Protection claims are decided against them, and these cases exceed 0.3% of the seller's transactions for the evaluation period. The two claims can be from the same buyer.

Examples

1. No Penalty

You're a Top-Rated Seller. You've cancelled transactions with five buyers within the last year, two of them within the last three months. Since you've sold 500 items in the last three months, only the two most recent defects count. So you're safe! You're defect rate is only 0.4%.

2. Non-Performance Penalty

You've also had five defects within the last year, but only managed to sell 398 items in the last three months. All five defective transactions now count toward your defect rate. Even though you've sold 1200 items over the last year and your defect rate is only 0.42%, the defects with five unique buyers are enough to get penalized for non-performance.

3. Loss of Top-Rated Seller Status

Your 500th sale for the last three months also turned out to be your third defect with a unique buyer. That puts your defect rate at 0.6% and costs you the Top-Rated Seller status. On the plus side, you don't have to worry about seller non-performance penalties as long as you don't get a defect with a fourth unique buyer during this evaluation period.

4. From Top-Rated Seller to Non-Performing in One Defect

I've sold 850 items in the last three months. I've just been hit by my third defect in that period—and unfortunately, all three of them were eBay Money Back Guarantee and PayPal Purchase Protection claims that were decided against me.

My rate of lost Guarantee/Protection claims has now hit 0.35%. Not only am I stripped of Top-Rated status, I've also lapsed into seller non-performance and eBay will decide how it wants to punish me.

Defects are clearly a huge threat to any seller. Since a tiny handful of defects can be enough to get even the biggest sellers slapped hard, you have to do everything in your power to prevent them. Here are some things you can do to avoid defects:

Keep Customer Service Efficient

Slow responses dramatically increase the chances of a customer getting upset, and if you don't respond to a buyer within three business days, then the case qualifies for the eBay Money Back Guarantee.

If you ever reach the point when it takes you more than three days to respond to all of your eBay messages, then things are way too bogged down. You need to start responding faster before your feedback score and defect rate are irreparably damaged.

Accept returns readily

Accepting eBay returns costs time and money, so you can't be blamed for wanting to turn down some, especially when they seem unreasonable. And you absolutely should if the buyer is completely out of their rights. But the more readily you accept returns, the better for your defect rate.

A buyer who has returned an item and gotten a refund from you has no grounds for claiming you did not resolve the situation. If you always offer to accept a return, you will be virtually immune to Money Back Guarantee and Purchase Protection claims.

Improve Inventory Management

The last step is making sure you don't have to cancel any transactions. If you always know exactly how much you have of every product, then cancellations should pose no problem.

Refunds

There are many reasons why you might refund a buyer: item not as described or damaged are just a couple. You will get a notification from eBay with instructions on how to proceed. There may be cases, though, in which you may want to issue a partial refund. Maybe the shipping was considerably less than what the buyer paid and you want to refund some of it, or something was missing from the order, and after communication with the buyer, they agree to a partial refund.

How to issue a partial refund

If a customer has returned an item through the returns program, or you authorize a return, you'll get instructions from eBay with a link. Here's how you can issue a partial refund through PayPal.

Log in to your PayPal account and find the transaction where you were paid. It will say "Payment from", followed by your buyer's name. Click on this link and you'll be taken to the transaction page. At the top right is a button that says "Issue a refund." Click that and enter the amount you want to refund in the total refund amount.

Chapter 12

You Can't Sell it if They Can't Find it

In 2013 eBay updated their search engine. The new eBay search engine is called Cassini. The idea behind this search engine was, like Google, to make it more relevant to what the customer is searching for. In a nutshell, Cassini wants to deliver products to buyers at the best price, from the seller who can provide the best service.

Here are some things you can do to give you a better chance of getting views and sales:

Use relevant keywords in titles

We covered this in chapter seven.

End listings and relist using *sell similar*

Since all fixed price listings are relisted each month, your listings don't expire unless the item sells or you cancel the listing. If I have listings that have gone more than a month with no watchers and very few views, I'll end the listings and re-list them. I always relist using the "sell similar" option. The Cassini search engine likes new listings, and using the sell similar option is the same as creating all new listings at once. I have never failed to get a boost in sales doing this.

Use the eBay catalog

This is helpful when you have a product that qualifies. When you use the "create a listing" button on your seller hub, a form will load and you see a field in which can enter the UPC, EAN, ePID, part number or product name.

Right category

Be sure your item is listed in the correct category.

Answer messages within 24 hours

eBay automatically gives you 5 stars on your communication DSR (detailed seller rating) if:

- You specify handling time of one business day and upload tracking information within one business day
- There are no buyer- or seller-initiated communications in eBay Messages, and there are no pending eBay Money Back Guarantee or PayPal Buyer Protection cases.
- There are no requests for contact information between you and the buyer.

The faster you respond to a customer, the more likely they are to buy from you. It also helps with your detailed seller ratings. This will help increase your buyer engagement on the listing once they buy the product and will give you a boost in search.

Start with lowest price

When you can, price your item the lowest or close to it starting out. Once you build up sales history you can start to raise prices.

Optimize for conversion

This simply means to take time to make your listing stand out.

Write good descriptions. Fill in item specifics, list features and benefits with bullet points.

Create combos – sell in lots (flea market lot reseller lot)

If you have a quantity of the same type of items, list it as a lot. Maybe you purchased a large lot of CDs at auction and there was a box of cassette tapes with it. It's hard to sell cassettes one at a time unless they're rare or new and sealed. Sell them all in one listing as a lot. Search for a **lot** of "*YOUR ITEM*" and see what other sellers are doing. It helps to put words like wholesale, flea market and reseller lot in the title.

Plenty of high-resolution photos

This is important. The search engines like clean, white backgrounds with no clutter.

Qualify for Google shopping

For your eBay listings to show up in Google Shopping, your listing needs to meet the minimum requirements and this varies per category. The bare minimum you need to have is brand, model and a product identifier (e.g. UPC, ISBN or EAN). You'll also need color, size, gender and Manufacturer Part Number (MPN) if applicable to your category.

Promoted Listings

I covered this in the *Sell it faster* section on the listing form. Promoting your listings at one percent can increase your sales. In the search results, promoted listings will be identified with the word "*sponsored*".

Chapter 13

Treasure Tales: $55.00 to $4025.00

I went to an auction of an estate owned by a college professor. There were around two thousand books in rooms all over the house. The auction was advertised online with over a hundred pictures. In the pictures I could see most of the books. I was interested in the office, which had hundreds of math, science and physics textbooks. These were used textbooks that are very expensive on Amazon and eBay.

When I arrived at the auction, all the books in the house had been boxed up in new Lowe's boxes. This was unusual because auction companies don't do this. That's the responsibility of the buyer. What I learned was that a buyer had asked to come to the house *before* the sale and box them all up. He was planning to buy all the books.

Auctioneers have a tactic they sometimes use to sell a room full of furniture or related items. They sell one item at a time but let the high bidder take their choice. They continue until all the items in the room are sold. None of the bidders know what the others are bidding on, and the auctioneer usually gets more money this way.

These textbooks books were in a bedroom office that included an antique bed, other furniture and twenty-five boxes of books.

The books were considered one item. The first item, the antique bed, sold for over $800.00. We all knew the bed was going first.

Then the bidding started again. I got the winning bid for $55.00 and chose the books. The guy that packed it all up had no idea I was going to get these. He had already bought all the other books in the house. The books in this office were, by far, the most valuable.

There were a total of 621 books in this lot. It took a lot of work getting them home, then sorting and listing. I sold 140 books on eBay for a total of $2922.71. The rest I sold to a used bookstore for $1103.00. Total sales: $4025.71. My profit after all fees, shipping and packaging costs was $3025.22.

More Treasure Tales

Here are some other gems I've found at auctions and what I sold them for. I've mentioned a few of these earlier in the book.

- A box of full office supplies purchased for $17.50. There was a micro-cassette recorder in the box that sold for $159.95
- A box of miscellaneous watches and jewelry bought for $5.00. There was a Staffordshire enamels hand painted trinket box from England in the box. I listed as a 7-day auction and it sold for $107.50.
- A "table deal" with three boxes of miscellaneous items for $10.00. In one of the boxes was a Polaroid land camera that sold for $77.00.
- Two Lord of the Rings Scabbards bought for $20.00 and sold for $450.00.
- 36 Mac Tools Cross Buffs – purchase price $35.00 for all

of them. Total sales of $675.00. I made a clear profit after all fees of $410.00 on these.

- A pick-up truck full of 1930s wallpaper bought for $80.00 and sold for $2200.00.
- And finally, there's the fundraiser inside sale I mentioned before. Two items bought for $10.00. Selling for $180.00 on eBay.

Chapter 14

Stuff I Thought You Should Know

I first started seriously thinking about this book five or six years ago. I made notes and wrote questions down. I saved Facebook posts. I ended up with notes everywhere: in my phone, handwritten notes and all kinds of folders and documents on my computer. I would run across something and think, "That would be good for my book". I managed to get a lot of the stuff into the book, but I'm still finding things. This chapter has some helpful hints that didn't fit anywhere else, or I just decided to put them here. Some of the material may have been covered earlier. These are in no particular order.

Marking a package as shipped

You need to ship within your stated handling time to avoid getting a late shipping ding from eBay. Here's what eBay says: "*Tracking information must be uploaded and validated by the carrier*". I've seen a lot bad advice on this subject in eBay Facebook groups. Sometimes things happen and you can't get a package to the post office within your handling time. When you print the shipping label, a tracking number is assigned and the buyer gets a notification that the item has been *marked as shipped*. This **does not** mean that you've shipped on time. The package must be delivered to the post office and scanned to qualify as having been shipped.

More listings/more sales

The more listings you have, the greater chance you have of people coming into your store or viewing your listings. The reason for this is a simple little link on every listing page that says "**see other items**." A buyer may have found one of your listings through an eBay search or Google search. Then they click the "see other items" link and start browsing all your stuff. After over twenty years I can tell you it makes a huge difference.

Global Shipping is selected by default when relisting

When you relist or revise an item be sure you look at the check box that turns on the Global Shipping option. This box is sometimes checked by default, even if the item was not originally listed that way.

How to find a listing when an eBay search doesn't work

Sometimes when I'm searching eBay listings, I can't find a listing like what I'm looking for. This is rare but it happens. eBay search results show you what *it thinks* is relevant, and sometimes you don't see all the listings. The answer is to do a Google search. If the listing has been set up right, often it will show up as a *Google* search result when you can't find it on eBay.

How to reprint a label

Sometimes you may need to reprint a shipping label. It may come out of the printer damaged, or the printer is out of ink, etc. In seller hub go the "Orders" menu and select "Shipping labels". The last label you printed will be at the top. At the far right you'll see a "Reprint" link. This will reprint the same label without charging you for it again. Clicking "More Actions" will give you a link to print another label. "Print another label" will allow to you print another, separate shipping label for the same order. You would only do this if the shipment is in more than one package.

VeRO (Verified Rights Owner Program)

Your responsibility is to know if an item you're selling is allowed on eBay. The VeRO program allows intellectual property rights owners to request removal of listings that infringe on their intellectual property rights, including copyrights, trademarks, and patents. Be sure you check this list. A couple of brands you can't sell on eBay are Velcro and Dunkin' Doughnuts. Do a Google search for eBay VeRO to learn more.

Sellers complaining of low or no sales

Every day I see Facebook posts of sellers complaining that their sales have tanked or they haven't sold anything in x number of days. The first thing they do is blame eBay.

As long as you have products people are looking for, you'll have sales. You have to change along with eBay. It's their site. Use the methods I teach in this book. Instead of blaming it on eBay, the first thing I would do is ask, "What am I doing wrong and what can I do about it?"

How does anybody make money selling stuff so cheap?

The short answer: They don't. There's no way you can make anything selling a two-pound book for $4.99 with free shipping, even if you paid nothing for it! There are several reasons. Sellers will sell something cheap, even at a loss, to get someone into their store. Wal-Mart sometimes sells a dozen eggs for thirty-three cents. Some sellers may just be obsessed with having the lowest price, no matter what. Another reason is that they've had it so long they just want to get rid of it.

Check your packaging by shipping it to yourself

To test his new business idea, the founder of Netflix mailed DVDs to himself in simple cardboard sleeves to see if they would survive. I sold replica vintage tin signs in my antique store booth and wanted to try selling them on eBay. I ordered some rigid cardboard mailers to test an economical, first class method for shipping. I took one with me on a trip to see my sister an hour and a half away and mailed it to myself from her post office in Paris, TN. It just so happened that the package got "lost" and took a very long route back to me. It went from to Memphis to California before finally making its way back to Tennessee a couple of weeks later. This was a very good test for my packaging. The sign came back bent, so the packing test failed. I abandoned that idea.

List every day

eBay likes new listings. Make a goal of listing *something* every day, even if it's only one item. If I haven't listed anything for a while, I always see a boost in sales when I start listing again.

Conclusion

There's not one single eBay book anywhere that will answer every question. You won't find answers to all your questions here. You just need to know where to go to get help. I've found that I can get the answer to almost anything on YouTube. If you have an unusual or fragile item you need to ship, just go to YouTube and enter "How to pack _____". There are literally thousands of videos about how and where to shop for eBay inventory. Here are a few helpful YouTube channels, some I've already mentioned before:

- Nesting Haven
- Lavender Clothesline
- Part-Time Pickers
- The Antique Nomad: I just discovered this channel. This guy travels all over the country buying and selling vintage and antique items. If you want to get an education of what things are and what they're worth, check him out.

Or just type "thrifting" into the search bar and enjoy.

Use a Google search. I use Google every day to get answers for all kinds of things.

Join eBay Facebook groups like *eBay Sellers Helping Each Other* or *eBay Sellers*.

I also want to invite you to my eBay Facebook page. I'm always adding all kinds of stuff. I have educational content, tips and tactics to help you with your eBay selling. You'll find the page here: https://www.facebook.com/ebaysellersresource/

If you've read this far, I sincerely want to thank for your investing your time and money in this book. If you've gotten some value, please head over to my Amazon author page and leave a review. My author page: stevenichols.us

My eBay user ID is flatbed-ford. (Be sure to put the dash in there).

Happy selling!

Steve

About the Author

After high school, Steve Nichols worked in the manufacturing industry as a supervisor and engineer. Then, after a career change, he spent twenty years in the trucking industry. Steve is retired and lives in Tennessee with his wife Rachel and their two pets: a white lab and an orange tabby. This is his first book.

www.ingramcontent.com/pod-product-compliance
Lightning Source LLC
Chambersburg PA
CBHW071422210526

45465CB00001B/489